And Then MAMA Said...

And Then MAMA Said...

Words that set my life alight

TUMI MORAKE

PENGUIN BOOKS

And Then Mama Said ...
Published by Penguin Books
an imprint of Penguin Random House South Africa (Pty) Ltd
Reg. No. 1953/000441/07
The Estuaries No. 4, Oxbow Crescent, Century Avenue, Century City, 7441
PO Box 1144, Cape Town, 8000, South Africa
www.penguinrandomhouse.co.za

Penguin
Random House
South Africa

First published 2018

1 3 5 7 9 10 8 6 4 2

Publication © Penguin Random House 2018
Text © Tumi Morake

Cover image © Kevin Mark Pass

PUBLISHER: Marlene Fryer
MANAGING EDITOR: Ronel Richter-Herbert
EDITOR: Lauren Smith
PROOFREADER: Ronel Richter-Herbert
COVER DESIGNER: Monique Cleghorn
TEXT DESIGNER: Ryan Africa
TYPESETTER: Monique Cleghorn

Set in 11.5 pt on 15 pt Adobe Garamond

Printed by **novus print**, a Novus Holdings company

MIX
Paper from
responsible sources
FSC
www.fsc.org   FSC® C022948

Penguin Random House is committed to a sustainable future for
our business, our readers and our planet. This book is made
from Forest Stewardship Council® certified paper.

ISBN 978 1 77609 334 2 (print)
ISBN 978 1 77609 335 9 (ePub)

DISCLAIMER
Every effort was made to credit the photographers whose photographs are included in this book.
In cases where a name has been omitted or the original copyright holder could not be traced, we request
that the relevant person contact us so that his or her name may be included in future reprints of this book.

Contents

Acknowledgements

I would like to thank Almighty God for this journey and opportunity. I have never walked alone – through every trial and triumph there have been angels beside me, in human and ethereal form.

Mpho Osei-Tutu, my long-suffering husband, my rock. Thank you for taking over our mini musketeers and everything else I had to drop to get this book done. Mme Mahlape, my mother. 'In-law' fell away long ago, I now use it purely for context. Thank you for reading this manuscript from day one, and for encouraging me when I became scared of my own voice. Ntate Tony, my cheerleader, thank you. Vonani, thank you for every call, every message, asking how the book was doing and whether it was done. You have no idea how that pushed me on my flattest days.

To my agents Osman and Shaaista, thank you for picking up my broken pieces and insisting I share my story. Lauren, editor extraordinaire, I hope you didn't lose any hair because of me. Thank you for your patience, insight and guidance. Penguin Random House, thank you for taking a chance on a voice that is often misunderstood, and being curious enough to risk an entire publishing deal on me. To every single person who sent me encouragement during my career and made me feel like I could have a story worth sharing, you too have had a hand in the birth of this book.

To Bonsu, Lesedi and Afia. I barely started writing about my life in this book; you will only find the bits that challenged, changed and grew me.

I hope you grow up to be resilient and forgiving of yourselves. Thank you for allowing Mommy her absences and for showering me with so many hugs and kisses. You've raised me more than you know.

Tebza, I hope I made you proud. You see, I am still a trier, moving with the confidence of a cockroach.

Dedicated to everyone brave enough to chase their dreams through treacherous waters. Keep swimming.

1

Ke na le kamore ko ga Mma

(*I have a room at my mother's house*)

When my mother faced challenges or felt like she had been painted into a corner, she would say, '*Ke na le kamore ko ga Mma.*' She was saying that as long as she had a home, she would survive. She also had a hand in building that home, and would tell me that to drill it into my head that you should invest in your family, in your home. That is how I was raised, by her and my grandmother: to value family and home above all else. Well, God came first, of course. That goes without saying.

Let me introduce myself properly: *Ke Mokgwatlheng wa mmathari ga e tshwarwe e sena shokwe, o nthapelle ke sa robetse, fa ke eme ga ke sa na thapelo.* That is our family totem greeting, which warns the listener to pray while I am sleeping, because once I am up, prayer isn't going to help them. Yup, that's me. Never catch me when I'm alert. Your ancestors may find themselves negotiating with mine for mercy. In other words, do not take me on. Our clan is peaceful, but once you have wronged us, pray we make peace again or you will feel our wrath.

I am a Motswana girl, a thoroughbred, if that matters, who grew up on the dusty streets of Thaba Nchu in the Free State. I was born Relopile Boitumelo Morake. Relopile Boitumelo means 'we prayed for joy'. When I see people smile or laugh in my presence, I feel I have lived up to that name. Relopile is a rare name; I have never met another. Boitumelo is as common as John; throw a stone and you'll hit a thousand of us. I was born in Moroka

Hospital in Thaba Nchu, where my mother worked. My upbringing was divided into three parts: I started out in a nuclear, white-picket-fence home in my early childhood, then was raised by my grandmother in my formative years. The last few years that needed adult supervision were taken over by the single parenting of Mama.

My father was a cop, but an underground ANC member. My mother was a nurse, also with political undertones. They were each highly intelligent, highly decorated firebrands. They met in the late 1970s in Thaba Nchu, when my father and a friend went to fetch a blanket my mother had borrowed. On the first visit they found my mother, but she had left the blanket elsewhere. On the second visit, my father went back by himself and left with the blanket and a phone number. Apparently it was love at first sight. Unbeknown to them, my dad was already a good friend of her sister's. He only discovered this when he went to see my mom, and there was my aunt. He asked her what she was doing there and discovered he had been dating his friend's sister.

They got married and had one child, me. We moved to Taung while I was a baby, as my father had been transferred to a police station there. I was far too young to have memories of the time we lived in Taung, but I remember we stayed in the police barracks of the Imperial Reserve when we moved to Mafikeng in my toddler years. My memories of life with my parents as a married couple are sporadic. They used to host small parties from December to January to celebrate our birthdays. First up was Mama, on 21 December, followed by me on 22 December, then my dad on 2 January. We used to hang out in the back garden, on the veranda overlooking the mulberry and apricot trees.

I played by myself a lot, letting my imagination run wild. I would often refuse to go to bed alone, however, and they would take me to their bedroom and let me fall asleep there before carrying me to my room. My eldest half-sister, Disebo, lived with us when she was in high school and I was in nursery school. I recall a lot of breakfasts with everyone around a little square table, Mama in her starched, pure-white nurse's uniform with maroon epaulettes, and Dad in his green cop uniform and hat. Most of my memories of Disebo take place in the mornings, perhaps because she was a teenager, so I saw very little of her. She and my mother clashed as well, so her living arrangement with us did not last long. Interestingly enough, though, they became close when Disebo was an adult. In fact, my mother ended up having a better relationship with Disebo than the one I have with my sister even now.

My parents had a close circle of friends and we often had people over. It was too good to be true, and maybe that is why it did not last. Unlike my parents, I was not very social, and as much as there were children in that neighbourhood, I enjoyed playing by myself and paging through books. The one time I did decide to go into the street and join the kids from the neighbourhood, I climbed high up a tree along with the other kids, then went a little too high, lost my footing and came crashing down, ass first. I landed so hard I saw stars, and it felt like my stomach had gone into my chest. I heaved, but no sound emerged from my throat. Eventually I found my voice and wailed. I do not know how my mother knew what had happened, but she was there. My butt had literally turned purple and blue from the fall, and I got an earful from my mom as she carried me home.

I remember my mother as the disciplinarian. I was scared of her. But my dad was my best friend. I even named him 'Tumi wa (of) TTA' (Tswana Territorial Authority), and I was 'Tumi wa Imphiri' (a shortening of Imperial Reserve). My dad took me on drives and to watch soccer. He was a huge fan of Bloemfontein Celtics, as are most Mangaung-borns. I would sing Phunya Sele Sele songs and fell in love with soccer. On Sundays, my dad would put me on his lap and read me the *Sunday Times* cartoons. For the longest time, right into adulthood, I would go straight to the cartoons when I opened the paper. *Blondie, Dennis the Menace* and *Redeye* became my Sunday staples. I would miss my dad a lot when he was away, and Mama would attend all my school events. I don't remember my father ever being there for those.

We shared a lot of laughter and quality time at home, just the four of us. For all his absences, my dad remembered many milestones and funny moments of my childhood. My mother was always surprised at the things he would recall, things she had completely forgotten about. That man's photographic memory is quite entertaining. We would visit Bloemfontein often, where I looked forward to seeing my dad's parents, who were already quite old. I also enjoyed seeing my half-brother, Tonono (his given name is Sesing, but nobody ever uses it). I adored him so, and he always had time for me. In fact, knowing that I had a brother and two sisters (Disebo and another older sister, Mathapelo) in Bloemfontein made the trip that much sweeter. They were children from my father's previous marriage. I was my mother's only child, and my father's last-born at the time. I never understood why we couldn't all just live in Mafikeng together.

Mafikeng was the capital of Bophuthatswana, a homeland run by a semi-dictator. I knew none of that, as a child. I learnt our national anthem, which was about how great it was to live in Bophuthatswana: 'Lefatshe leno la borrarona' (Our forefather's land). The first verse was all about how this land was God-given and received without any bloodshed. The bullshit we sang in the homelands was sad propaganda. My favourite, though, was the unofficial anthem 'Go Monate Mo Bophuthatswana' (It is wonderful in Bophuthatswana). We would sing it at the top of our voices in nursery school, and if you thought you were too good for Bophuthatswana, you would never come right.

Everyone admired the president – Lucas Manyane Mangope – but my parents openly disliked him, and he would become my first experience of having an enemy. As a kid, I just thought he made funny speeches and people made fun of him for being president of the homeland of Bophuthatswana. He gave everyone a thirteenth cheque in September and was called a visionary for the Batswana people. He once threatened any-one carrying a South African passport that they would be kicked out of Bophuthatswana so that they can go and be South African elsewhere. As a puppet of the apartheid government, he was nevertheless strongly opposed to Bophuthatswana being assimilated back into South Africa. There were attempted coups in the late 1980s. My father tells me of this man, P.J. Seleke, who knew where my father stood politically, but had no evidence to support this. This Seleke character was the police commissioner at the time. He hated my father, even threatened his life. My father escaped with his life but lost his freedom when he was detained in 1988.

The nightmare actually began in 1987, when we left the Imperial Reserve and relocated to the suburbs: number 33 Dan Pienaar Road in Golfview, Mafikeng. We moved there with my father, but that didn't last long. My parents were being watched and followed. I was none the wiser; some hushed conversations would just happen around me. My father constantly had intel of being targeted, as many of the people he worked with were either being jailed or killed. In December 1987, he went underground and my mother and I fled the city. My mother woke me up in the middle of the night and my father took us to the train station. That was the last I saw of him for some time.

It was my first train ride and I had the time of my life. The vendor selling snacks and drinks told my mother that he would keep me safe, and I went from cabin to cabin with him.

I had no idea how much stress my mother was under. We went through Kimberley and disembarked in Bloemfontein, where we were picked up and taken to Thaba Nchu. The usual roadblock was there between Botshabelo and Bloemfontein, manned by South African police. Those cops didn't just ask for your driver's licence; they shone their torches in your face and searched your car. The drive from Mafikeng to Thaba Nchu had always been an odd experience. In the 1980s, Thaba Nchu and Mafikeng were part of Bophuthatswana, not South Africa, but Bophuthatswana comprised disconnected areas of land separated by hundreds of kilometres. So to get from Mafikeng to Thaba Nchu, we would drive from Bophuthatswana to South Africa and back into Bophuthatswana again. It was nonsensical, really.

The traumatic thing about this trip was that I had always lived with my parents, and now circumstances dictated that my mother leave me at my grandmother's place. Upon her return to Mafikeng, my mother was arrested for treason. She never spoke to me about her time in prison. The only story she told me was of how, after her release, she demanded her job back and her six months' salary because she had been wrongfully arrested with no conviction. Mama wasn't quite the same after this experience. She seemed a little hardened.

Meanwhile, my father had been smoked out of hiding by the news of my mother's arrest, and the next time I saw him was when he was behind bars. So, essentially, Lucas Mangope had both my parents jailed, leaving me virtually orphaned at one point in my life. Mama was not active in the struggle, just outspoken and well-read. My father, on the other hand, had been fingered as a spy and was wanted for treason. This old man Mangope, this apartheid puppet, as my father called him, had robbed me of my family unit. It was a shock to the system. Suddenly I was using public transport and living with people I usually only visited for a few days at a time.

One advantage was that I was surrounded by playmates. I quickly adjusted to sharing space, although it took a while to get used to sharing things like my toys and books. Fate had landed me in a decent family home, where my mother had grown up, just along the N8. I crossed that road on foot for most of my childhood. As in, if you are driving through a *dorpie* and you see a young girl dash across the road, you calm your 120 km/h self down to the recommended 60 km/h.

A little village called Ga Ramakgari was home. All the grandchildren called our grandmother Mma, mother, like her own children did. Most of us were raised by her anyway. I didn't really have friends in our neck of the woods, save for Mmami, whose grandfather drove us to school every day. My full-time friends were my cousins; everyone else I interacted with at school.

Often we would walk back home after school, and since my eldest aunt, our Mamogolo, worked in town, I would pop in to see her. She would show me off to her colleagues and give me ice-cream money. Even when she fought with my mom and they weren't talking, I would still go and visit her, much to Mama's chagrin. Mamogolo was the black sheep of the family, a tiny, no-nonsense woman who had run away from home and had zero fucks to give. I loved her energy. She was the smoker, the drinker, the loudmouth, and she laughed as easily as she cursed; I think I 'inherited' my foul mouth from her. My favourite, and my father's best friend. She spoke without fear or favour and people loved her because she kept it real. Also, she didn't bother with places she wasn't wanted. She would happily tell you to shove it, and then move on, never bearing any grudges – the beef was squashed where it started, and if you were not over it, that was not her problem.

The difference between her and Mama was that Mama was not controversial for controversy's sake. She had her moments. My aunt was the entire moment. This woman encouraged me to stop being at the mercy of people's opinions and taught me to have a thick skin and be comfortable in it. She was also the sexiest of my aunties. She wore the tight dresses and the cool pants; she was just so damn hip.

When she lost her son, my cousin Tumi, in 2006, it was the closest I felt death play near me. We had planned an outing on that weekend. It was such a confusing experience for me, and I was too shocked to cry. Mamogolo was never quite the same after that. Her resilience faded, although the cheek was still there. She had punchlines for days. When I fell pregnant with my third child in five years she laughed and said, 'Yeah, let them know you don't sleep in tights. You are married, after all; those aren't three choice assorteds.' When she passed away in 2015, I felt like I had lost Mama all over again.

My grandmother's house was also home to Mamane Fola, my mom's younger sister, whom I feared. I could count the number of times I had seen her smile – particularly at me. I felt like she cut me down every chance she got and, as a child, it hurt. I could not understand what I had done to offend her so much. Even now, as a fully grown adult, I am slightly uncomfortable around her. She is such a loving human being, and over the past few years she has been there for me in more ways than I can count, but that eight-year-old girl in me still cowers in a corner around her. Nevertheless, she practically raised my younger sister when Mama was struggling with her mental health, and for that I am forever indebted to her. She taught me the importance of protecting your space and keeping people at arm's length when necessary. Most importantly, she taught me to be there for family at all costs.

I owe my resilience to strong women like these. Controversial, prayerful, conservative and loving. I was shaped by all the women who raised me when I lived with my grandmother. In that time, 1987 to 1992, I was moulded by the hands of my aunts.

I hated winter in Thaba Nchu. I am not hyperbolising here. I do not have happy winter memories. Thaba Nchu is a stone's throw from Lesotho, the very same Lesotho that has a *ski resort*. And the flatulence of Lesotho winters lands squarely in the face of Thaba Nchu. My grandmother's humble abode sat at the edge of this location. On the other side was a veld that led to the mountains. There was a long trench that directed water from higher ground over the rainy season to avoid flooding. The water would remain there long after the rains, and cold winds turned it into an inappropriate air conditioner with no off-switch. Going to the toilet was a challenge. The sub-zero clutches of winter would grab at our tiny buttocks as we sat on the loo, and the long drops were overly airy in my opinion (except in summer, when the ventilation was most welcome).

My grandmother's armour for the wintery war was a thick layer of petroleum jelly to lock in the heat. Yes, my people, Vaseline, standard. On warmer days, when we played outside, the Vaseline would attract so much sand that you would be peeling cakes of it from your legs and feet. Covering that additional skin of Vaseline was enough clothing for at least three other children. Mobility was comical, and peeling those layers off was an event.

Bath time was torturous. My grandmother had these cylindrical paraffin heaters that we used to heat our washbasins. There was the supernova – the best heater in the house – which everyone wanted to bath with, but there was only enough space next to it for one basin, so it would be about the luck of the draw in the mornings. I was notorious for over-sleeping and almost never drew luck in this draw, so I had to live with what I got. There I'd be, kneeling in front of my plastic basin while crouching as close to the heater as possible. My skin was always cooked by the end of winter. And if an adult walked in and found you that close to the heater, you would feel a hard smack to remind you to keep a safe distance.

The speed of our baths was record-breaking, and obviously many a spot was missed. Punishment would arrive in early spring, when spring-cleaning included your body. Nobody got involved in your cleanliness until spring. Then the infamous orange sack would come out. These would be in high supply thanks to all the oranges we'd bought to keep the vitamin C going. This painful exfoliator was the enemy of any black kid unfortunate enough to have a mother or female relative who saw the extra-dark hue of missed winter washes on you. In my case, it was my cousin Galo or my Aunty Benni.

Aunty Benni is our youngest aunt, the baby girl of the family, and my first nanny. She occupies a special place in my heart. My favourite of all her phrases is: 'Hoe gouer hoe beter, hoe later hoe kwadder.' Now, I don't think 'kwadder' is a real word, but in essence she was saying, the sooner you deal with it, the better. Aunty Benni has a wicked sense of humour. She would make fun of our grimy necks and say, 'Bona moruti ka koloro' (Your necks are so dirty, they look like a priest's collar). It hurt, but not as bad as Galo, who considered bathing us a hateful chore. She grated our skins with that orange sack, and I hated her every winter.

But I loved school in winter; it was the only good thing about the season. Tlotlanang, having once been a whites-only school, had great facilities. Hey, man, our current government could learn from those apartheid guys; they took care of their people. Each classroom had coal heaters that filled the room with heat from wall to wall. I looked forward to it every morning.

I had no shortage of kids to bond with. I spent most of my childhood with my cousins: four boisterous boys, and two girls who visited occasionally. We would put two bricks at opposite ends of my grandmother's house and play soccer. I was a mean goalkeeper and defender. On rainy days we would sneak off to the veld just outside our home, where we would collect some clay. Then we would mould objects out of the clay – like people and cars. Every time my eldest son, Bonsu, complains that he's bored, I lament the price of privilege. On other days, we took the clay and moulded it into little pellets, placing them on the edge of a stick and hitting each other with them. It was painful and got us into a lot of trouble because, inevitably, someone got hit too hard and the tears would flow.

My cousin Rea and I were closest in age and played together a lot. We used to get into such trouble, and when our grandmother got a hold of us, we wished for death over that torment. My grandmother seldom hit us. Instead, she would lock you in between her legs and pinch you between the thighs. It. Hurt. Like. Hell. We were all quite light-skinned, so our thighs would be red for a couple of days after. The more serious transgressions were handled by a belt called *kgwele* – shoelace. The most ironic name any weapon could have.

We plotted against that thing. Our earliest plan was to hide it so that my grandmother would never find it and would therefore give up on it. When that didn't work out (it was always found), we formulated a better plan: we stole the belt and threw it away. We were a little overdramatic in this regard, throwing it all the way out in the veld. It had taken us months to gather the courage to steal it after we learnt where she kept it, but it was such a happy day when we made it disappear.

We managed to avoid getting into trouble for a week before she discovered that the belt was missing. Rea put on a wonderful performance of fear and dread when my grandmother went to fetch it. I had to hide the way I was dying with laughter. Of course she couldn't find it, but she didn't suspect Rea because, well, he was already wailing as if he were about to get a lashing. Then I started crying too, because the idea that she might pinch me if she found out that I was involved was too much to bear. The case was never solved.

I learnt early on how to defend myself, because when fights went down, they were physical and they were brutal. I also learnt how to take pain, to grin and bear it. On two occasions I hurt myself badly, but I soldiered on. The first time, I fell on an old wire fence and the spike of the fence dug into my leg. We pulled it out and it came away with flesh. I was bleeding profusely. Rea, who was with me at the time, reminds me even today of how much I bled and how the only thing we panicked about was the belt-hiding we would get, because we weren't allowed to play at the *kraal* anyway.

We covered the wound with dung and sand. It was only discovered the following morning at bath time. My aunt cleaned it out with methylated spirits and cotton wool. It stung like hell and, surprisingly, was not infected and never went septic. I dared not tell them I was at the *kraal*; the only explanation I offered was that I fell. That was it, and that was enough.

The next time I should have gone for tetanus shots and first-aid 101, but didn't, was when I went too close to a fence that was still being put up and walked into a wire that pierced about six centimetres into my skin. My uncle Ngwako pulled it out and stopped the bleeding. I cried a little, but I dealt with the issue and moved on. These hurts prepared me for life's little knocks. Now, instead of sitting and crying, I find a solution. Wallowing is exhausting, and there's no victory in it.

Whenever my mother came to see me in Thaba Nchu, I would know she was there from the sound of her loud, deep voice reverberating all the way up the road from my grandmother's house. It was the most soothing sound I knew. She would either be howling with laughter or sharing anecdotes with my grandmother. My heart would burst with joy and I would run to the house. Her perfume always hit me first, a strong, spicy scent that smelt like a combination of her own scent, her lotion and the perfume itself. Everything she used was perfumed. I would get a big kiss from her and a demand for all the school gossip. And a mini tongue-lashing for all the trouble I had got myself into while she was away, but there was never much; the most consistent complaint was that I was lazy and stubborn. I hated domestic work – it just wasn't a skill set that came naturally to me. And in my defence, I always completed all my chores, grudgingly or not.

My favourite gift from my mother every time she came to visit was my reading matter, from *Archie* comics to Ladybird books. She had me covered. I was affirmed by my mother's interest in the things I loved. When I developed a fascination with archaeology, she brought me books on that topic. Whenever she saw an article related to archaeology, she sent it to me. When I started painting, she bought me my first watercolour set. And she always had copies of *Reader's Digest* for me, because I would read the jokes and anecdotes at the bottom of the pages. She noticed these things without me telling her. I felt loved.

Without fail, my mother came to collect my school report at the end of the academic year, and every year, without fail, I had merit awards to show her. She also phoned every week and would visit whenever I was on holiday or when she had leave days. I would get bonus visits if there was a funeral in the family or a traditional ceremony. So I saw my mother frequently, even though I lived with my grandmother 500 kilometres away. She would spend a couple of days with us and then sneak off when I wasn't paying attention, as she hated saying goodbye to me. I would start sobbing and follow the car out of the yard, and I think she couldn't bear that. I don't think my mother ever got used to me crying. Even when I had to have an injection, she would leave the room.

If I knew she was coming, I would sit at the back of the house watching the N8 for her car. As soon as I saw it approaching from the intersection, I would run to open the gate. It was such a happy feeling, better than Christmas. I would go to the car in search of loose coins, and then my cousins and I would run off to buy snoek and *vetkoek*, and peanut cones. Or we would cross the N8 for sweets – those black round sweets that everyone called 'nigger balls'. We didn't know that the word was a racial slur. In fact, I only learnt about the meaning when I started listening to hip-hop in the 1990s.

Mama's visits changed when she met Papa Henry, as I called him, a big, dark guy from Johannesburg who carried wads of cash and always had an entourage. She would come to town, but she would stay in a hotel. The plus side to that was that she would pick me up, along with my cousins, and let us spend the day at the hotel – either the Thaba Nchu Sun or the Naledi Sun – where we would gorge on junk food and play video games. I loved how my mother's visits became a treat for everyone when she hooked up with this rich man. It wasn't just about her spending time with me; all my cousins and I got spoilt. She was very clear on that principle: if I got something new, everyone got something new. If I got to visit nice places, I had to share the experience with my cousins. It broke the mould of a spoilt only-child and made me a sharing and generous kid.

My mother divorced my father while he was still in prison. At the time, I thought it was cruel. I did not get the sit-down and explanation that I see kids getting nowadays when there is a divorce on the horizon. I was not told anything at all. My aunts from my father's side came to visit in Mafikeng while I was on holiday there. I use the term 'visit' loosely. They came over and spent a tense day with us. Mom sent me on a playdate and took my aunts to Rooigrond prison without me. Everyone looked unhappy, and I chose to keep my distance.

Something was not right, but nobody was crying, so I knew it wasn't a death thing and asked no questions. Thereafter, I suddenly stopped going to visit my father in prison. I missed him dearly. He would write me and I would resent Mama for not taking me to see him. Papa would make papier-mâché frames and put his picture in them for me. I felt sad for him, for his struggle.

I only found out that my parents were divorced when I went digging in my mom's papers for a notepad, which I needed for my usual art rounds. And there, in the drawer, were the court papers. I read my father's name – Diratsagae Abram Morake. I read her name – Tebogo Joyce Ulenda Morake. I saw my name – Relopile Boitumelo Morake – and the words 'full custody'. At the top of the paper it said 'Decree of Divorce'. It had gone uncontested and my mother got pretty much everything. Just like that, my already shaky world collapsed under me.

I cried by myself. I was also scared: my life would never be the same again. I thought about my father's strange question during my last visit, when he asked if any men had been visiting our house. I had overheard

Mama speaking about being followed, so I wasn't sure if he was referring to that. I hadn't met Papa Henry yet, and I do not know if she had already been seeing him. I had so many questions for Mama, but how could I ask her about this without getting into trouble? And why did nobody think that I needed to know? Where the hell was my father supposed to go when he came out of jail?

I avoided Mama like the plague that day. Eventually she got irritated and sent me to my room. I obliged. She died never knowing how I had found out such a huge thing all by myself, or that I had to carry it all alone, to decipher it and find a way to live with it. My mother never told me about the divorce, and I never confronted her about it.

In the meantime, my mother fell pregnant. She and Papa Henry had moved in together. He struck me as a kind man and made me feel like I was his daughter. Papa Henry travelled a lot, and what I liked about his presence in my mom's life was that even if Mama couldn't pick me up in Thaba Nchu, he would send drivers to take me home to her over the holidays. He fit neatly into my life, like a stand-in dad while I waited for my father to be released.

Papa Henry made our lives easier and never made me feel like he was trying to supplant my father. I spent most of my school holidays in Mafikeng, but Mama and Papa Henry would also take me on holidays to different parts of the country, and my cousins would come along. We got to stay in hotels and lodges and were really spoilt. He was like a permanent Father Christmas (with a belly to fit the Santa image). So the prospect of a baby was exciting; I was hoping for a little brother.

My younger sister, Vonani, was born a month before Nelson Mandela's release in 1990. I had not seen my mother for months during that time, because Johannesburg was a volatile place to be, let alone Soweto, where Papa Henry was from. For the first time in my eight years of life, I was not an only child. I had been dethroned by another girl and was most upset.

I had nightmares in which I saw myself decapitating her like a Barbie Doll. I was resentful because she was keeping my mother away from me and everyone was going on and on about her. But when I eventually got to travel to Soweto with my grandmother, I fell in love with the beautiful bundle in my mother's arms. I thought that, naturally, this meant I would be moving back in with my mother, because we were now a family. So I cried for hours when I was sent back home, leaving the perfect family behind. My mother, her new man and their baby. I felt left out and rejected. Papa Henry had been good to me, but I wasn't his kid. And now that he had one, I got shut out. I did not get to drown in self-pity much, though, because my cousins kept me busy.

Then Papa Henry was killed in a collision somewhere outside Mafikeng, before Vonani's second birthday. The man he was travelling with escaped with just a broken leg. It was a huge shock and my mother was devastated. I had had a premonition about his death, but I was just a child and did not dwell on it. For years since then, I often wonder why I knew, where that vision had come from.

Papa Henry's family took everything they could claim belonged to him and literally abandoned Vonani and my mother. All Mama was left with was the house and my baby sister. Even the car Papa Henry had bought her was taken. My mother had to pick herself up and start again. She could not cope, and Vonani joined me at my grandmother's house. I do not blame Mama for giving us up for a bit.

My sister became *my* baby. I even helped potty-train her. She destroyed so many of my books and toys, but I was happy to have a sibling around – at least initially. A lot of the responsibility of watching her was thrown at me. Vonani was added to my long list of daily chores.

My grandmother was the queen of consistency and routine. We watered her garden every evening, after fetching water for the next day. Lunch boxes were prepared the night before, and she checked them every time. We never had a helper. On weekends we cleaned that house from top to bottom, and washed our school uniforms. What we did after that was none of the adults' concern. This had always been a great reward, until I lost my freedom of movement to my sister. If the boys got up to anything away from home, I was left out of it because 'Who is going to watch the child?' I resented my family for doing that to me.

However, the *worst* thing that happened to me as a pre-teen was grow-ing breasts. The boys started refusing to play with me because I had breasts. It was like some kind of confirmation that I was no longer one of them. This was rejection of the highest degree, and I had to resign myself to playing with my little sister and burying my head in books. The only time

I saw my female cousins was when their parents came over, so it was usually this boys' club. Although I would stay with Vonani, my mind would be in the faraway lands of the books I was reading, which landed me in hot water every time. By the time I was eleven, I could babysit any small child, because I had been raising my little sister, and in many ways I had grown up too. By then, I wanted out of Thaba Nchu. I was a pre-teen bookworm who was misunderstood by her family, plus I wanted to live with my mother.

In 1991, my father was released from prison, two years after I had found that letter. Before he headed to Bloemfontein, he came to our house. I was so happy, my heart almost exploded. I was at the house opposite ours, visiting my friends, when we saw my dad at the gate. Words cannot describe the emotions that came over me – I was so excited to see him free from that horrible place. He looked good, happy. At least, his eyes did. I jumped into his arms and stayed there for a while. He stood with me on the side of the street. We talked about how well I had done, what grade I was going to. I introduced him to my little sister, and I think I saw sadness come over him then, but he brushed it off. My mom wasn't home, so we went inside for a bit.

He looked so good, my dad. He was wearing formal shoes, formal pants and a shirt. It felt natural that he should just stay so we could continue as normal. My stepfather was dead; I did not see what the hindrance was.

After a while he said he had to go, as he would be travelling to Bloemfontein. My voice cracked. My heart cracked. I turned away. My father asked me to walk him to the gate, so I did that. It was the longest walk of my young life. I waved goodbye, putting on a brave face. Then Mom's car drove in. Dad didn't turn back. She walked in and instead of greeting her, I shouted, 'Papa is out of jail!' I did not wait for a response. I ran to my room, sobbing. In that moment that I told her, I saw the words 'Decree of Divorce' in front of me and realised I was not getting my family back. I sobbed so hard; I was heartbroken. The happiest event had conveyed the saddest news to me. Vonani, barely two at the time, was a welcome distraction, because she just would not leave me alone. I swore I would never get married for as long as I lived.

2

Just bring me a matric certificate

Finally, the time came for me to move in with my mother. We moved one street back from the home I had once shared with my parents, to 31 Jan Smuts Avenue; a place I would call home until I left for Johannesburg in 2000. Every holiday before that happened, I would ask my mother when I would be moving back home to live with her. In 1992, over the school holidays, my mother took me to Connie Minchin Primary School in Mafikeng to write an entrance test. I knocked it out of the ballpark with a short story about a girl who had to learn about road safety. The teacher made a comment about my excellent writing.

A couple of months later, a letter arrived at Tlotlanang School in Thaba Nchu. I was asked to pick it up from the principal's office. It had the Connie Minchin Primary School stamp on it, and I could not resist opening it on the way home. I remember seeing 'welcome' and '1993'. My heart jumped with joy and tears welled up in my eyes. I could not stop smiling. I tried and failed miserably to mask the fact that the letter had been tampered with, claiming to have received it like that. I don't think they believed me, but I didn't care – I was going home! I would live with my mother and my sister and be happy for the rest of my life!

This was the second happiest moment of my life – getting a Dino Baby bike as a toddler was first. Somehow, I couldn't imagine that I would miss my cousins – I was just looking forward to having some space, a room entirely my own for quiet time where I could read without interruption. Most of all, I would get to sit on the sofa! After all those years of my bum growing numb or my leg falling asleep under me, sitting on that damn carpet, I would now live in a home where I could enjoy the cushy comforts of a couch. And my ass would no longer be at the mercy of the elements when I needed to do my ablutions in cold weather. Most importantly, nocturnal toilet visits would be a corridor away. Life was looking up. The catch, though, was that I did end up missing my cousins. We played together from the time we woke up till the time we went to bed. In contrast, there was a big age gap between my little sister and me, *and* we were trying to kill each other half the time.

Months after moving back to Mafikeng, I fractured my wrist in a park fight. I was a cute little light-skinned girl who probably looked like an easy target, and I don't think anyone expected to encounter a girl who could give as good as she got, even in a fist-fight. Although I spent most of my time at home with my books or in front of the telly, sometimes I would hang out with the neighbourhood kids in the park around the corner. It wasn't a big park – the size of two average yards, with two sets of swings, a roundabout and a seesaw. But I loved going there for the company. Life was a little lonely without my cousins.

One of the boys started a fight with me when I dribbled him and embarrassed him with a 'spy two' – an 'ishibobo' to the born-frees, or a nutmeg. I had played soccer for ages in Thaba Nchu with boys and so had no fear playing against them. In fact, I had decided I was a born defender (and went on to play in that position at Wits). But this boy got mad, and made a nasty remark, so I punched him in the back. It was game on. When I went in to kick him in the nuts, he grabbed my ankle. I fell hard and landed on my wrist.

By the time I got home, my hand had turned various shades of blue and looked like a blown-up latex glove. My mother took one look and knew it was serious. She could not understand how I had waited until she had knocked off hours later instead of phoning her at work to say I was hurt. The real pain hit me when a drunk doctor attended to me and covered my entire arm in a cast. It was heavy and ridiculous. After a disastrous few days with this cumbersome thing, my mother took me to a different doctor. He looked at the X-rays and asked why I had been given such a big cast. The plaster of Paris had to be sawn off. All that movement and vibration aggravated the discomfort, and for the first time I was hysterical with pain. This doctor was very upset with the shoddy job that had been done. He fit me with a more practical cast that did not restrict my elbow.

I never told on the kid who'd fought with me. I said I fell off a swing. A likely story; my mother had seen me fly off the swings mid-air before. The injury earned me serious street cred. I went back to the park with my cast on and was officially one of the boys. Nobody messed with me after that. I was not the last to be picked for the team, and I no longer worried about my developing body getting in the way of being considered part of the gang. I wished those cousins who wouldn't play with me because of my breasts could have seen me, playing rough with other boys and kicking ass at soccer.

Mama and I got on like a house on fire. I always felt that she was in my corner. She could read my moods and never downplayed my stress. When I did not want to go to school, she would happily write me a letter explaining my absence. As long as I delivered the results, I could get free passes. Because of this, I choose not to be too hard on my own children. They can go wild at home; it is a safe haven for bad behaviour and venting. When they go out into the world, however, they are exemplary children. That's how they earn their hall pass. They are generally pleasant at home, but if not, we let them finish their nonsense before we admonish them. I never want to fail them when it comes to being who they are in the world. Home should be your place to let loose. All that pent-up delinquency should be exhausted there so that the world gets something more manageable to deal with.

What I did not realise about Mama, though, was that she was battling her own demons. In retrospect, I now understand that the times she would lock herself away in her room and forget to eat were red flags. Sometimes she would have these maniacal spurts of joy where she would blow all her money or stay up into the wee hours of the morning, cleaning the entire house and yard. Then there were days when she just wasn't up to any conversation. I figured these were standard mood swings. A few years down the line, this behaviour would be diagnosed as manic depression.

Mama hardly ever hugged me, but she gave me lots of kisses. She kissed me as she left for work every single time. In high school, I would die of embarrassment when she would still want to kiss me goodbye. She also went through a neck-biting phase. She was naughty, that mommy of mine. (My daughter also loves giving me kisses randomly; it's like she knows.) Mama was a highly decorated nurse; one only had to look at her epaulettes to know that she had mastered just about every discipline in the field. Her favourite was midwifery. Psychiatry came a close second. Mama also had a soft spot for old people. She wanted to take care of them and loved having long conversations with them. She hated seeing old people as vulnerable and lonely, and frequently spoke of opening a home for the elderly, where they would be well fed and have a medical-care facility so they wouldn't have to make clinic trips.

On days when she wasn't in the mood for work or when her job was particularly demanding, Mama would say, 'I chose this job myself.' What she was saying was that she had to take responsibility for her choice and show up for work, despite the difficult conditions, the uncaring nurses, the demanding patients and the lack of financial reward. I would listen to her complaints, laugh and commiserate, but her response was always the same.

Mama's after-work routine stayed pretty much the same. When she got home, the first thing to come off would be her flesh-coloured stockings – she would head straight to her room and sit on her bed to take them off. I would make a beeline for her bag. A warm scent would emanate from it when I peeked inside – spicy perfume mingled with a hint of Granny Smith apples and original Stimorol. Those things still make me miss her every time I have them.

As a teenager, I spent a lot of my time massaging Mama after she got home from work. I loved it. It was our bonding time. My sister would join us on the bed and also ask for a massage. Mama would burp every time I massaged her, as if all this gas had built up inside her while she was doing her rounds at work. I would massage it all out, and in the process learnt a lot about tension, knots and stress.

It might not have been safe, living on our own in Mafikeng, but I think Mama's deep voice kept us from harm all those years. What ill-intentioned criminal watching a house with three women in it wouldn't turn on his heels if he heard a baritone belting a hymn from within?

Rather, the dangers we experienced were the result of political unrest. Change was coming and things were unstable, going from bad to worse. Sometime in the last quarter of the school year in 1993, someone began coughing uncontrollably during choir practice. The next thing, the entire back row started coughing. Our choir teacher got annoyed, thinking the kids were messing around. But in no time the entire room was coughing, and then the school bell sounded. We were all ushered to our classrooms. Next, we heard gunshots. Our parents were phoned. We were scared, but not sure what of. But nothing happened, and we all went home. The police had clearly managed to put out whatever political fire was about to start ... for the moment.

It would be a year later, on 11 March 1994, that the real scare would come. South Africa was due to have its first multiracial, democratic elections, and Bophuthatswana would no longer be an independent homeland, but would be reintegrated into South Africa. Lucas Mangope had announced that Bophuthatswana would boycott the elections. There was a huge uproar, and Mafikeng became unrecognisable: grey smoke, more cop cars than I had seen in a long time, and giant army vehicles. I didn't know what the hell was going on.

Mama said Mangope was about to see his arse. Looting had begun, and Mama made it very clear that I was to stay at home and indoors. Schools closed for a week. What we did not know was that, in true apartheid-puppet style, Lucas Mangope had enlisted the help of the Afrikaner Weerstandsbeweging (AWB) in dealing with the rioters. We soon ran out of basic groceries and all the shops were closed, so Mama and one of her neighbours decided to try the little shops in the surrounding suburbs. There were no other cars on the road. I think we should have taken that as a hint to make a U-turn and make another plan for food. We could hear gunshots, but we all assumed that they were coming from town. According to the news footage, it was like a warzone out there.

What happened next gave me newfound respect for my mother. As we drove up the main road towards Riviera Park, a car with armed AWB men came hurtling towards us. The guys were shooting at random from the car windows. I heard screaming. My mother shouted for me to duck, and all I heard after that was the screeching of wheels and the gunshots getting louder. I did not stay down; my curiosity got the better of me. Fear is as slow as my metabolism – it's always the last thing on the scene. My mother swerved into the next road and turned at every corner that came up. She did not know if we were being followed, and she was not going to wait to find out. We reached a dead end, and my mother and her friend just started praying. We parked there for a while; nobody said a word. I was scared then, but also impressed with my mother's driving skills. (I had seen her drive like a Formula 1 driver once before, when my sister had an epileptic attack while we were shopping. The speed with which we got out of there and to the hospital was dizzying.)

Eventually my mother started the car and found her way out of wherever we were. There were no other cars or people in sight. Everyone was probably in their houses, glued to their TV screens, waiting for the next explosion of violence. A chill came over me when we watched the news later and saw how a policeman had shot some AWB men at point-blank range in town that same day. They had apparently been shooting at rioters, and I wondered if they were the same guys who nearly took us out that afternoon. For the longest time, I also asked myself why my mother allowed me to watch such things.

As a child, I was outspoken, yet afraid of corporal punishment. Hurting myself when I was playing was one thing, but receiving intentional pain was something else. I feared reproach generally, because unlike a fall or an injury, a lashing was a torment you had to sit through until it was over. I could not imagine anything worse. Hence, I was a good girl, just loud-mouthed. And stubborn. I think my determination to be articulate and express myself was considered worse than being a naughty girl who came home after dark. My aunts couldn't take it: to them, a child who talked back was worse than one who broke windows. Their authority could never be challenged by a child, and they made that abundantly clear. That just did not work for me; I was not good at being aggrieved and keeping it to myself.

When I was in trouble with Mama, she would call me by my name, 'Boitumelo', and admonish me with 'jou ma' (your mama)! Or she would say *'Boitumelo o dira mmago'* – (literally, 'What you are doing is your mother,' properly translated as, 'You are out of line.') Her choice of words would crack me up for obvious reasons.

My mother was firm when she needed to be, and made sure she calibrated my level of fear of her. I once saw a hideous woman on TV and said, 'Who's the ugly bitch?' without thinking. That day, I had to wash my mouth with soap; it was the first and only time in my life. On the other hand, she gave me licence to go full sailor when *she* was in the firing line.

Mama had been getting rides home with this doctor and, in my ignorance, I saw nothing wrong with it. They may have had a 'thing', but I never saw anything untoward. His unfortunate wife called and demanded to speak to the person sleeping with her husband. She was already ranting. I assumed she was speaking about my mother and hung up the phone. When the relentless, angry wife called again, my mother picked up. The wife told my mother that *I* was sleeping with her husband, and did she know…? My mother told the wife not to call our house again; if she couldn't control her husband, it wasn't our problem. But the woman kept calling back, and Mama said I should answer the phone and swear at her.

Kid-in-a-candy-store moment! I get to swear at an adult? In front of my mother? With no punishment? Yes, please! I was sixteen, with the vocabulary of a gangster-rap fan. When I picked up the phone, the woman asked if I knew about AIDS. Ah man, I pulled out my best hip-hop hits and some Afrikaans just for control. The *taal* was still second nature, living in Mafikeng and all. This was the one and only time my mother dropped the mommy hat and decided, fuck it, this is war. But after that, she stopped getting lifts from Dr Naughty McNaughty.

Mama used to tell me, 'Just get me a matric certificate. Then you can sleep with all the men you want to.' She was in no way encouraging me to be loose, but she certainly wanted me to keep my priorities straight. She wanted me to be independent, especially financially, and well-read. My mother's love for education and her deep desire for her daughters to grow up well-educated and empowered was never in any doubt. She would tell me about married women with a low level of education who were treated as intellectual inferiors by their educated husbands. Mama's good friend, the late Judge Mpho Ngwato, was a single, beautiful, articulate and successful woman. Mama loved taking me with her to visit Judge Ngwato so I could see how a single, strong woman did it. Mama respected women like Mpho because they didn't let men rule their lives.

My relationship with men changed with life experience and age. I did not have the energy for the bickering and politics girls indulge in. I liked the playfulness of guys and their straight talk. If they don't like you, they avoid you; they don't pretend to like you but then talk rubbish about you behind your back. I struggled to fit in with girls, because their cliques had too many rules. There was a freedom attached to being one of the boys: it established that I was off-limits as a sex target. I learnt to read guys better – if someone had hungry eyes for me, I knew to run in the opposite direction. I was somehow incapable of being mean, but I was the queen of duck and dive. Nobody to compete with, nobody to impress. Hanging out with guys just made sense, and so I spent most of my teen years as 'one of the boys'.

I was mayor of the friend zone for so long that coupling wasn't a priority, but as my hormones kicked in at full force, it became awkward. These were my boys; I couldn't deal with feelings *and* camaraderie. Inevitably, I would have a crush on someone who desperately wanted me to hook them up with someone else. Being one of the boys sucked on such occasions. Or, one of them would get drunk and start getting handsy, making things awkward the next time the gang hung out. I began to withdraw a bit from that and found myself hanging out with some badass girls. It wasn't as enjoyable as hanging with the guys, but it was great to know that no matter how wasted we got, none of them would try to push themselves on me.

I made friends with this guy, Maestro. At least that's what everyone called him. I have made great male friends throughout my life, and Maestro was one of them. When he came to our high school, nobody messed with him – everyone feared him. I don't know what drew him to me, but he took me under his wing and that was that. He may have liked the fact that I was not scared of him. Not because I was a badass; I just hadn't been given a reason to be.

Maestro was my disciplinarian. He once caught me smoking and smacked the cigarette out of my hand. He threatened to go home with me so I could explain to Mama what he had caught me doing. Maestro cared. I dated his friend and broke that friend's heart, yet he still kept me as his little sister.

On one occasion, Mama attended a funeral in Thaba Nchu and I had to stay behind because of school commitments. Maestro kept an eye on me in her absence. He invited me over to a house he had been house-sitting with his friend. A pool table, drinks, company: I was not going to say no to that. I had got up to shit; Maestro knew about it and wanted to understand why I was acting in a way that wasn't me. I had cut school a couple of times, was smoking cigarettes and, on occasion, marijuana, (Marijuana was tragic peer pressure. I did not really enjoy it, initially.) And I was getting booze from our older friends. I was being a rebellious teenager on the surface, but hurting beneath it all. Maestro knew my personality; he knew how bright I was, so why was I working so hard to be a bad girl? I came up with bullshit excuses about being lonely and my parents splitting. He lectured me on choices. Then he said he was going to take a bath, and invited me to join him.

Now, let's get one thing clear: I loved Maestro and he loved me. But with a brother? Again, he wanted to know why I expected to be pushed into bed at every turn. I told him guys were generally pigs. He laughed and told me to stop being silly and join him in the tub. I stripped down, he stripped down, and we jumped in.

We had a long conversation about my life with a single mom and how much I missed my father, and getting caught up in the wrong crowd. I asked him why people were so scared of him. He laughed it off. People weren't scared of him, he said; they were scared by stories about him.

I believed him about as much as you believe that I bathed with him and nothing happened. But nothing did. Even though guys had tried to sleep with me purely because we happened to be in the same room, this one treated me like it would have been incest. I think I stopped writing men off that day and considered marriage for the first time. If I ever got married, I wanted a guy who would treat me like Maestro did: hard enough to keep me in line, but soft enough for me to know it came from a place of love. Maestro had a heck of a temper on him, but was actually a gentle soul who laughed easily. He was the brother I never had.

Having Maestro as my friend, however, lulled me into a false sense of security around guys. For a while I did not consider them a threat, and I knew that if any of them messed with me, I could just tell them Maestro was my brother, and that would generally convince them to back off. But Maestro was not my bodyguard, and the day came when I wished he was.

I met the loveliest young man from Malawi, and he took me out for a movie. Such a gentleman. It was May, so the days were getting shorter. About ten minutes from home (I was walking home on my own), it began to get dark. There was a group of guys walking behind me. I was not scared or nervous; this was my 'hood. I had walked this way in darker conditions without fear.

Tonight would be different. As the men drew closer, I could smell the sweet booze on their breath. One of them came up behind me and started getting fresh. I handled him with humour and a clear message that I was just trying to get home, but that I was happy to walk with them. I decided to take a well-lit route, but this guy started pushing me towards a darker path. His friends shouted for him to come, to stop wasting their time. He just kept pushing. Fear gripped me and my mind raced.

I mentioned Maestro, but he was unknown in these parts. The guy started to get more violent, and I tried to make a run for it. He tripped me. I landed hard but fought back. I was doing quite well and screamed to draw attention. As I screamed for help a second time, he grabbed my throat, choking me. I could not breathe. I could feel my heartbeat and his other hand tugging violently and hurriedly at my trousers. I felt light-headed and began to recite the Lord's Prayer in my head. As I was about to lose consciousness, cold air pierced my throat. He had let go and his friend was on top of him. I could barely make out what they were saying, but they were arguing.

My rescuer walked me home. He kept asking if I was okay, saying his friend was drunk and stupid, and asked if I was going to call the cops. All I wanted was to get home. I lied about where I lived and went in the gate at a neighbour's house. Halfway to the door, I turned back. The guy was gone. I waited until I could be sure he was really gone and then ran home. When I opened the door, my mother was already gearing up to shout at me. She said, 'Boitumelo …', but when she saw me, she was gutted. I must have been a mess. The guy's grip on my neck was clearly visible; his nails had even dug into my skin. The scars on my neck took a long time to fade. My pants were dusty, my hair was a mess and my eyes were puffy.

In a broken voice, Mama asked me point-blank if I had been raped. I told her what had happened, and before I'd even finished, she asked me what direction the men had walked in. She took her butcher's knife and got in her car. It was hours before she came back, angry and frustrated. She clearly had not found them. In true black-mother style she came down on me like a ton of bricks: how irresponsible I was to be out that late; why didn't I get whoever I had been out with to take me all the way home; how much worse this could have been. I knew it was all love, all fear.

I was so damn sorry. I learnt a big thing from that experience: the Lord's Prayer yields results.

Mama never found out when I was raped for real. I could barely say it to myself, and could not imagine having to tell it to my mother. It was not as violent as when that guy attacked me on the street, but it was a frightening and traumatic experience. I made the usual mistake of being overly trusting. It was a murky situation because it was no secret that I had a crush on the guy. I wasn't lusting after him; I just found him dreamy. Turned out he was a hellish nightmare.

He had let me borrow his belt when my baggy pants were falling down at a concert at North West University. He said he would get it back at the hair salon where we both worked part-time, but then he asked for it at the end of the performance. Sometimes I want to go back and bitch-slap my teenage self for agreeing to go back to his room with him. However, this guy was friends with my cousin's boyfriend, so I had no reason to think I was in any danger with him. Plus, he had shown zero interest in me, so I thought I was happily sitting in the friend zone with Mr Dreamy.

When we got to his room, he told me to sit down and then put on a Jodeci CD. In the hair salon, every time Jodeci's 'Freek'n You' came on, I lost my mind. When K-Ci did his hook, I would do my sexy jam – not for this guy specifically, but I would dance like a video vixen with a mop for the entire salon staff. It was just my way of clowning around at work.

So this guy played that song in his room and told me to take off his belt. I laughed and said no. He said he wasn't playing. His face changed. I got up to leave, but he raced me to the door. My hand was on the handle. He put his weight on the door and locked it. I turned and looked at him; where was this game going? He started kissing me. I giggled. As he kissed me, it became apparent to me that I had no feelings for him, but he was acting like this was some kind of aphrodisiac. He pulled back, I apologised, and he went back in for the kiss, harder this time.

He was an older guy, at university. I was a fifteen-year-old high-school girl who pretended to have more experience than I did. He was grabbing me everywhere, while I was pushing his hand away. He grabbed for my pants, yanking his belt off me. Then I realised he really wasn't playing.

I turned my head away from his face and asked him to stop. He tried to shut me up with kisses. I said I couldn't breathe. He raised himself off me a bit, but when I shifted my body as if to get up, he began doing what he had intended to do all along. I desperately said I was a virgin, hoping he would stop. He didn't. He had stopped responding to me. I started crying. Screaming did not occur to me; I was searching my mind for ways to escape.

The dorm was very noisy, and I was swimming in a haze of confusion. When he had my underwear off and I felt his skin against mine, I begged him to use a condom. I said please so many times; I am a virgin, please, I don't want to die. Without getting off me, he reached into his drawer.

He broke me, he ripped me; I bled. Throughout this experience I was pushing my arms against him, but he kept his body firmly on mine. When he was done, my eyes were stinging from sweat and tears. He combed my hair, dressed me. No conversation. No apology.

He walked me back to my friends. I was surprised they were still there; I felt like I had been gone forever. All I wanted now was to go home. I began to walk off the campus, to find whatever last taxi would be out there. On my way to the gate, my cousin's boyfriend spotted me and offered to take me home. He said I must have had a hell of a party because I looked finished. I was finished, all right. Soulless.

When I got home, I did not have my key and it was long past my curfew. My mother opened the door. I hoped she would slap me or scream at me, at least. She took one look at me, said nothing, turned and went to her room. I started crying. I went through a plethora of dark emotions. I threw my underwear in the dustbin. I don't remember wearing those clothes again. I was raped in baggy jeans and a baggy shirt. At my least sexiest or suggestive. By a guy I liked. I questioned myself. Had I sent him the wrong message? What explanation could I give for being in his room? Why didn't I scream? By asking him to use protection, didn't I somehow give in and make it consensual?

After that, my school marks dipped, my ability to be truthful began to falter. I couldn't be alone any more; I needed constant company. I wish I had met Maestro before this happened – I would have asked him to panelbeat this guy for me, while I watched.

About a year later I shared what had happened with a neighbour, after she noticed me avoiding the guy at that same salon, which I had left. When I took a gamble and told her, she said he had done the same thing to her. I asked her if we should go to the cops. She said, hell no – her father would kill her if he knew she had been anywhere near the university. Also, how would we explain waiting this long? So we never spoke about it again. It took me years to get over it, but I dealt with it and have since been able to speak about it without going back to that moment and reliving the experience.

In 2016, I unthinkingly told this story to a journalist, thereby turning a profile piece about my work into a rape headline. I have a problem when I get too comfortable with someone. Comfort is like a truth serum for me, and once I trust you, I will sing like the proverbial canary. The journalist and I were talking about being a woman in South Africa and taking up traditionally male roles. Khwezi, somehow, came up. The name Khwezi – a pseudonym given to the woman who accused Jacob Zuma of rape – was back on everyone's lips. Her passing and the spate of violence against women in the country seemed to have hit a nerve.

I realised, after the interview, that I should have uttered the 'off the record' disclaimer, but I was not coming out consciously. It should have been more conscious, more considered, because when people share their pain, they invoke other people's forgotten or existing pain. I spoke about the normalisation of things that constitute rape in this country. Why did I bring it up? Knowing that I have family and friends who read the papers…?

Firstly, what touched me about Khwezi was that the shame clung to her, not Zuma. That bothered me. Secondly, to ask why I would speak about being raped implies that the shameful act should remain hidden and that I have a stake in that shame. No, sir. No. I am at a point in my life where I will share my truths and own them. They may not be absolute, they could possibly incite consequences I did not plan, but I cannot take responsibility for how people react or feel. The over-polite political correctness of this country has taken it backwards in many ways. Truth loses flavour and power because we are so damn busy sugar-coating it. Grown men who should be able to tell the difference between Tinder and the workplace are getting away with atrocities because we sugar-coat their actions, then sweep them under the carpet.

The blame is put on the women who step up and speak out; their integrity is questioned rather than the perpetrators'. I have spent so much time in rooms full of men wondering, statistically, how many of them are rapists, molesters, harassers or woman beaters. If I stand a high chance, statistically, of having this happen to me in this country, can you imagine my anxiety at the idea of releasing my daughter into that self-same world? So every time I see her stand up for herself, I am reassured that she'll do just fine.

In 1999 I applied to Wits University – I did not apply anywhere else, as I had no interest in going anywhere else. I was so cocksure of getting in that I told everyone I'd be going to Wits. The only murky bit was what I was going to study. I loved art, I was an art student and graphic design tickled my fancy. That, and textile design. When the Independent Examinations Board returned our portfolios after marking, I sent my portfolio to Wits as part of my application. So, there I was, ready to study towards an honours degree in Dramatic Art or a degree in Fine Arts. My dreams had nothing to do with television. I always saw myself becoming a theatre star and writer.

Mama, a single parent of two on a nurse's salary, could not afford to send me to university. There was added pressure: I needed to make sure I worked hard enough to at least obtain a bursary. My father was still rebuilding his life, even though it had been ten years since his release from prison. I was prepared to take whatever he could give, but I was not holding my breath.

I spent most of my matric year living alone or at my best friend Gago's parents' place. Mama was in and out of hospital with manic-depressive episodes and not doing well. She had blown all her money on Lord knows what. Her generosity reached epic proportions when she was on a high, and nobody saw it necessary to say no when she gifted them precious possessions. At some point, even our VCR disappeared, and she was unperturbed when I asked about it. I knew she had given it away.

That was the year I could have made all the wrong choices and done nothing better with my life. I am grateful that I wanted more for myself. I also knew that my mother still had high hopes for me, and I wanted to live up to them. I wanted to give her a reason to pull herself together and get better. Though I still loved the occasional party and I had a love life, they became less important than getting through school.

As much as I have taken so much good from my mother, I have also tried to learn from her mistakes. One of her biggest weaknesses was financial management, which was exacerbated by her mental illness. She was always hiding from people and companies to whom she owed money. It was her undoing. Some people joke about that kid who gets told, 'Tell them I'm not here,' when debt collectors are knocking at the door. That kid was me. We'd play that awkward game of statue when we were lucky enough to see someone coming through the gate: TV off, complete silence. They knock, go around, look through windows. You don't breathe. Then they leave, and there is relief. My mother's bank card lived with the *mashonisa*. Things would get so bad, we would be living on hospital food she brought from work. (This is probably the only reason I don't hate hospital food.)

The tragedy of my mother's life is that when she was with my sister's dad, she lived a lifestyle way above her salary bracket. When he passed away and his family took everything – his business, cars, furniture – she started from scratch without scaling down. I don't even know if she owned the house we lived in or if she was renting it. I just know it was the final sign that her life had a major crack in it and something had to be done. We walked away and, like Lot, we never looked back.

That used to be another one of my mom's favourite things to say: '*Shebella pele wena, o tla fetoga pilara ya letswai*' (Eyes forward, otherwise you will turn into a pillar of salt). The one thing she always had money for, though, was our school fees. I am also grateful that she had the presence of mind to let her siblings help her raise my sister, otherwise she would have been even worse off. I hope my sister doesn't resent her for doing that. I had been there; I got it. I think watching my mother struggle with money scared me into being conservative with how I spend mine. I have never cared much for keeping up with the Joneses, because I don't know where or how they got what they have.

I had to figure out a way of getting to Wits. I think it was October when I travelled to Johannesburg for the interview process. For the life of me, I cannot remember how I got to Johannesburg. I just know I travelled with a friend, whose older sibling lived in Johannesburg. I was dropped off outside a huge, imposing building I would later learn was called University Corner. We were divided into groups and given info packs. It immediately felt like home. All my nervous energy left me, as if it had found another place to vibrate. Wits felt like it held a lot of promise for me.

Some hefty white lady interviewed me. She scared the bejeezus out of me, as she looked hard and I could not read the expression on her unsmiling face. Her glasses magnified her view into my skull. Any kind of eye contact with her made me squirm; it was as if she could see right through me. We had a long conversation about how demanding the dramatic arts degree would be. She wanted to know how I planned to survive in Johannesburg and where my finances would come from, because the demands of the degree left no time for part-time jobs. I thought to myself, *Nobody told me this was a rich-kids-only degree.* But I was unshaken in my resolve to ace the interview.

I did not express my desire to perform, though. I stuck to my writing and stage-design interests, throwing my love for creating in the mix. She asked how much theatre I consumed back home. I had had zero exposure to theatre except for a Kwaku Ananse play that Aubrey Sekhabi had directed at the Mmabana Cultural Centre, which had made me want to be in the arts more than ever. I started to wonder if this was not going to go well for me, but I wanted it so badly. I left with a sliver of hope when, before dismissing me, she said she liked how I expressed myself. I returned to Mafikeng, excited at the prospect of being in that great place where stars were made.

Back in Mafikeng, I knuckled down and got through matric, which was purely due to the glory of God. I had no adult supervision for the most part, with my mom being in and out of hospital, so obtaining those school results and even showing up at school literally came from me. Mama had been readmitted to hospital because she was simply not coping, and the psychiatrist was trying to figure out her medication. She seemed far gone, but somehow I still believed that my mother would heal from this illness like any other. It was just taking longer than usual. My sole focus now was to finish matric and finish well. I did not want to find myself stuck in Mafikeng the following year. I had a strong feeling Johannesburg would be a brand new start for me. I needed it, but without a matric exemption it wasn't going to happen. Overnight I had to become a self-sufficient teen – eat right, wash my uniform, get my work done and show up for class. Thank God Vonani was living with my aunt in Thaba Nchu by then; I have no idea how I would have coped with having to take care of her as well. I went into those exams with one aim: university entrance points. Mathematics was the biggest threat to the dream, so I joined study groups and watched some study-guide show on TV.

Eventually Mama came back home, and she seemed to be doing well enough in the last quarter of the school year. When matric graduation rolled round, she was there. I had been praying she would be in her best mental state. I was honoured to have been asked to give the all-important valedictory speech. Although it had been a rough two years building up to this, Mama was intent on not letting me down. She was so happy and relieved that I had made it this far, and she'd never had any doubt that I would pass matric. She arrived early for the ceremony, dressed to the nines, face made up, hair done.

In my speech, I took a moment to thank her for getting me through the rough and tumble of high school, and especially for doing it all single-handedly. She covered her face with her programme. I knew I had made her cry with happiness. I pointed her out, and the crowd turned to look at her. Mama's time in the spotlight. That was one of the proudest moments of my life, and I shared it with her. I do not think I had ever told her how proud I was to have her as a mom until that day.

3

We can live on
bread and water

Mama used to say that she would happily live on bread and water as long as Vonani and I were educated. She held educated women in very high regard, and I wanted to be that: Mama's graduate daughter of whom she could be proud. In January I received a letter from Wits: I was two points short because of my maths grade. Go figure. Maths had stopped being my friend in Grade 8, when I discovered that boys could be more than just friends. I had to travel to Johannesburg to write an entrance exam to be admitted for first year. Again, a glimmer of hope in the grey cloud forming overhead.

Before, Mama had managed to get me to Johannesburg, but this time I was on my own. I arrived at Park Station in downtown Johannesburg and had to figure out my way to Wits from there. Now, Park Station is a meeting point for travellers coming from all corners of South Africa and surrounding borders via train, taxi and bus. It is an overwhelming bustle of people and the Tower of Babel of African languages. It is also a feeding ground for petty thieves. I was just a small-town girl trying to make her way to a university somewhere near this place.

Park Station is where God showed me that I have never walked alone, and never will. As I made my way out of the bus terminal with much trepidation, I bumped into Kwaku, a former senior from high school, whom we had lovingly called 'Chief'. He had just seen somebody off, and get this: he was heading back to Wits! I couldn't make this stuff up if I tried. We walked to the campus together, and he literally stayed with me until I was settled in my residence. Kwaku was one of the undergraduates assisting new students who were coming to campus for various rewrites. I sorted out my accommodation and found a friend to guide me to the exams hall the next day. I cried tears of relief and sent Mama a very happy SMS to tell her I was safe. That night I couldn't sleep and stayed up playing *Snake* on my Nokia. In the morning, I wrote my entrance test – it was *such* a breeze – and made my way back to Park Station, safely escorted by Chief. His girlfriend, who was in my year, had already been accepted into Wits and he had every confidence that I would be too. If his being sent to me as a guide was anything to go by, I had this one in the bag.

A couple of weeks later I received my welcome letter. I. Was. Ecstatic. Mama and I cried and prayed. All she had asked me for was a matric certificate, and here I was, upgrading that to a degree. I told her I would ask my father for funding, as he had promised to help me with my tuition when I finished matric. She told me not to hold my breath. Either way, I had already applied for a bursary and had no reason to believe I wouldn't get it. Mama promised to go on early retirement so that I would have the money I needed, but I said no. My little sister still needed support, and with my brains, there was no way I would not get that bursary.

When the news arrived, however, the wind was knocked out of my sails: the bursary would pay only 50 per cent of my fees. Mama would have to come up with the rest. Worse still, when I arrived at Wits, I was told I had to pay for the room that had been reserved for me, because the bursary did not cover my accommodation. Then another angel came to my rescue. My schoolmate, the same one who was dating Chief at the time, allowed me to squat in her room for a while. Her roommate was quite accommodating, and for a week, while trying to figure things out, I had a place to stay. Mama was already drowning in debt, but she took on more and got me into that residence. And that, ladies and gentlemen, was the tricky beginning of a journey that would bring me closer to my dreams. I became a Wits student.

Wits University was a bit of a culture shock for me. It was the first time I was surrounded by openly gay folk who weren't camp and colourful. There were more white people than I was accustomed to being around, and the Indian students were way less conservative than what I was used to back in Mafikeng. Everything moved at a dizzying speed, and I did not have a mama to go back to every day. The amount of partying as well – my goodness. I like a good time, but once in a blue moon. I felt like I had arrived at party central. I made friends easily, but mostly with people in my class. I made a friend for life when I met Solanche Aaron, a strong girl I nicknamed Pocahontas. Her mother, Lynn, is a beautiful coloured woman, and her father an understated Indian guy. Solanche speaks like a posh white lady. She's a typical South African, with all kinds of idiosyncrasies that turn stereotypes on their head. When I met her, I started to think what a headache racial classification must have been in the bad old days of apartheid. South Africans are such a wonderful mixed bag of goodies that classifying and separating must have been like sorting rice grains by brand. I met an Afrikaans girl who confessed to having a crush on a black guy but being afraid to do anything about it because our pubic hair freaked her out. Those tiny tight curls on the chest were too much for her, and she didn't think she could cope with seeing them on intimate areas.

I loved the openness and honesty of drama school. Nobody was afraid of their truth, or at least that's how it looked from where I stood. Being in drama school felt like a calling, and I began to find freedom in my own truth. I had had a brief sexual encounter with a girl in high school, and for the first time I was unafraid to share the story and speak to lesbians about what it meant to them to navigate this world as openly gay. I had never been around 'out' lesbians before. That kind of acceptance meant a lot to me. I had spent so much of my life trying to fit in, with family, at school, in society, and here I was in a space that encouraged otherness and freedom.

Ironically, it was a nightmare to try to fit in anywhere in the entertainment industry. My accent was too black or not black enough. I was not fat enough to be Mama Themba, but not thin enough to be Thembi. And my favourite: not township enough, but then again, too rural. I stopped trying. Whoever wanted what I was offering would have to come and get it. The big difference, I found, is that, at drama school, we were not a group of insecure people with something to lose. Drama school was a group of invincible artists who loved their craft, and we knew no one could take that away from us. We all knew why we were there. In contrast, the entertainment industry is a mixture of people, some of whom know that they have longevity, others who do not know when their luck will run out, and those who know their meal tickets have expiry dates because they aren't the best.

In my first year, I studied performance, design, television and writing. Over time, I realised my passion was for writing and performance. University allowed me to discover an artistic scope within me that I had no idea existed. Wits was also where the comedy bug bit. During orientation week, John Vlismas had rolled in with some comedians at lunch time, and a few friends and I decided to check it out. I had never laughed so hard in my life. The stand-up-comedy format was one I was not familiar with at all, and I was fascinated. After the show I went up to David Kau and told him that one day I would do what he did up there. Cocky. He said, sure, do it. He didn't even maintain eye contact with me, and I felt dismissed. Later, I reminded him of that day, but of course he didn't remember me. Why would he? Besides, I wasn't fawning over him like the other girls; I just wanted to know how I could get into comedy.

It would, however, be another two years before I actually got onto a stage and took a stab at it. For the moment, I stayed focused on drama school.

By the time we got into the swing of things in first year, I had already acquired a boyfriend. Yes, 'acquired'. I don't think Mike was actually interested in me to begin with; he kind of woke up one day and realised he was my boyfriend, and remained thus for two years. He was from Thaba Nchu. I had no interest in getting myself caught up in a mess with fast Joburg boys, so I played it safe. Mike and I were such a rough-around-the-edges couple. At one point he'd shaved my head and we walked around looking like skinheads. We played soccer, drank beer and shared what can only be described as colourful language. I spent more time in Mike's dorm than my own, and I was convinced that I had found my husband. We were possessive of each other, but he had a roving eye. I was a flirt, but he was a finisher.

I also met Mpho Osei-Tutu in my first year, and although I'd initially found him annoying, he became a part of my small group of friends and, well, we got along.

Towards the end of first year, I went home to Mafikeng over the study break. I opened the door, thinking nobody was home, when a putrid stench hit my nose. It turned out that Mama had not been out of the house for months. She had taken to her bed, and our neighbour actually thought she was out of town. Some food had gone off, she had not been eating and the house was falling apart. A leak had ruined the ceiling in the dining area, and the glass panes in the front door were broken and had been replaced with cardboard. The red *stoep*, which stretched all the way from the gate, was looking drab. I refused to believe that my world, as I knew it, was crumbling around me. I had never, in all the years I had known Mama, seen the place look so neglected. Years later, I would have disturbing dreams that we were back in that yard, everything fixed up, with Mama trying to get back into nursing. That darn gate would still be missing, but the *stoep* would be polished and shining, and the yard green, with a healthy rose bush. I have had these dreams for a long time, and each time I wake up with my heart racing. I don't know if it is because I still haven't come to terms with the magnitude of losing Mama and a home I once knew, or if I yearn for some kind of closure.

What broke my heart more than a broken home was a mother I could not recognise: her speech, her mannerisms, her lack of self-care. But when she saw me she lit up, and my heart lit up and that hope came back. I stayed positive. I told myself it was a rough patch that we would get over. I went to church that first Sunday and prayed for her.

Unfortunately, things did not improve. This was bigger than she and I could handle. I spoke at length with my uncle, who said he would fetch Mama and take her back to Thaba Nchu with him. I agreed. In fact, I was relieved. Mama had exhausted all her funds and could not account for a lot of her money and possessions.

When she finally did move to Thaba Nchu, there were still loose ends and missing items, including the bedroom furniture from my sister's bedroom and mine. Our house in Mafikeng? She had given it – yes, you read right, *given it* – to our neighbour a couple of houses down, who lived in an overcrowded situation and needed bigger accommodation. This was no life; Mama needed to be surrounded by people who could keep an eye on her.

My second year of varsity was difficult. Mama sank deeper into depression, and I would go weeks without being able to reach her. Nobody at my grandmother's house would know where she had disappeared to, because she would often leave at the crack of dawn. She had taken an early retirement package when she went back to Thaba Nchu, and offered me the money to help me with my Wits fees. I refused to let her pay the full amount; she could pay half, and I would demand the other half from my dad. Bad mistake – he never came through. Mama deposited a lump sum of money into my account. I investigated savings options and discovered unit trusts. In one of my bouts of responsibility, I took most of that money and invested it there. It earned interest while I figured out what I did and didn't need. I bought my first PC and a printer; the only extravagances I allowed myself. The leftover money came to the rescue for school supplies throughout the year. I didn't really have money sense, but I knew that I did not want to have financial worries. I had to push myself academically and could not afford to be distracted by my finances.

Emotionally, though, I was a wreck. Mike was losing interest and cheating on me. I had genuinely fallen in love with him, but he was still playing the field. Mama was not well, although she still managed to pull through for me when I needed it the most. A group of students were invited to Prague to perform *Venus*, a story about Saartjie Baartman. I was playing Saartjie.

Mama found out and made sure I got my passport, travel money, wardrobe and anything else I needed. She travelled to Johannesburg with my younger sister and cousin in tow, in some random guy's car. She couldn't come to the airport, but my friend Andile was there to see me off. I'd inherited Andile from Mike. He was tall, dark, handsome and chubby, and the friendliest guy you could ever meet. We hit it off immediately. Andile and Mike grew further apart as Andile and I grew closer. I had made a friend for life, and when Andile heard that Mike would not be seeing me off at the airport, he chose to do so instead. This is where I always note God's grace. At every turning point in my life, there is an angel, real-life, walking with me. Everyone else had family and friends seeing them off, and I had Andile.

Mike, however, barely had time for me in my second year and it ended badly, in Thaba Nchu, over the holidays. I had already found solace in a senior who resided on West Campus, and the break-up meant I would have even more time for him. Tall, handsome, charming, arrogant. What was there not to love? Our weekly date revolved around watching *Ally McBeal* and *Frasier*, and he read me extracts from novels like *The Great Gatsby* or books by random philosophers. It wasn't a relationship; it was a longstanding fling that lasted through three of his relationships. Ours was a simple understanding: we enjoyed each other's sense of humour, had sexual chemistry and enjoyed the same shows. And then it was done, with no hard feelings, no weirdness. Our favourite shows had gone off air and we had finally found ourselves in separate relationships worthy of our undivided attention. Academically, however, the emotional turmoil had caused me to lose focus, as was obvious in my results. I passed the year, but I failed one module.

I could not jeopardise my chances of graduating from university. I went back with blind determination to make my third year my best academic year, but I had no idea how I would pay my fees. Mpho and I started dating, and he quickly became a great shoulder to cry on. I moved out of res and in with my cousin in Chiawelo, Soweto. I had never been to Soweto except as a kid, travelling with Mama from Mafikeng to Diepkloof, where her boyfriend was from. I only remembered how incredibly scared I was of being jackrolled or stabbed. I grew up in the homelands, and the picture painted of Johannesburg townships was bleak. My only memory of Soweto was during the uprisings pre-1994 – and that was a scary time. I had been a sheltered girl from Bophuthatswana whose dad was in prison because the guys who ran this part of town had jailed him. Now, I would have to commute from Soweto to Wits early every morning and return in the evenings.

By 2003, I was deeply in debt to the university. I had applied twice already for a loan from Wits, and had now run out of lifelines. I did not even have enough to register for a new year, even if I could raise the money I owed. Eventually I received a letter saying I would not receive my results or be readmitted until I had paid my debt. I had seen it coming, but it still left me demoralised. I could not come this close to my degree and have the opportunity snatched so easily from me. I wanted to do this one thing for myself and my mother, so I decided against staying in Thaba Nchu. I had a better chance of finding my way into the industry by living in

Johannesburg. I did not remain in my rut forever, but there was no support system at the university to help debrief or support students who found themselves in this position, it seemed. I was on my own, but I wanted that degree.

What it took, in the end, was six years of building a career and making a life for myself forged from blind determination and an insatiable hunger to make a success of myself in Johannesburg. In 2009, after giving birth to my first child and meeting my accomplished in-laws, I decided to tie up loose ends. I had repaid my debt to Wits in full and had a small window of opportunity left to go back and complete my degree. I did not need to go back for the skills, as I had learnt all I needed from working in the industry. However, I wanted to avoid the 'But Mom, you never finished your degree, why should I finish mine?' argument that could happen with my son in the future. Also, I wanted to finish the degree for my mother, so she could say she had a graduate in the family. I wanted to gift my mother this degree. She had loved my overconfidence in applying to a single university, and I had to deliver.

To get back in, I had to write a motivational letter describing my reasons for returning to the institution. I kept it simple: 'As you can see from my results, I was a dedicated student and I was forced to end my studies by circumstances beyond my control. I am already gainfully employed in the industry and feel I could make a meaningful contribution to the faculty.'

I was accepted back in no time.

My first day back was daunting. You could smell the 'the world is yours' promise in the air. But I felt my age. The fashion, the lingo and the energy of the campus made me feel old. I sat in class with wide-eyed twenty-year-olds with idealistic views of the industry they were about to be thrust into. I used to look at Wits as the beginning, the springboard. I used to pause all those years ago and look up at the tops of the buildings in awe and disbelief that I was privileged enough to be there. Now, I was trying to figure out how long it would take before I could roll my eyes and say, 'Screw this, I make a ton of money; I don't need to be here.'

One of the girls in my film-studies class said I should really consider getting into stand-up comedy. At first, we all thought she was joking. Then someone told her I was a headliner. It was a sweet moment, but I was due for a good helping of humble pie. Good thing I love pie.

It was wonderful to go back to basics, to interrogate my work. I once again watched films critically, and wrote essays dissecting them. I was studying the world I was working in and thinking critically about it. I wrote a play, short stories and a script in record time. I was meeting deadlines and going to the library. I just did not remember having so much reading to do before, my word! I don't know how I got through it all the first time I was at university. Robust conversations around representation and narrative agency gave my brain the wake-up call it needed. I still had it. The cobwebs and dust were cleared off my academic mind. It was, in more ways than one, the most sober experience of university!

Getting into my car after class, memories flooded back of walking to the residence with friends. Memories of a time when going home meant three times a year by train or taxi. University was a very different experience now that I had money and prestige. I could load my student card and just swipe my way through campus. Nor was I working hard to impress anyone in the faculty in the hope that they would earmark me for their work. I felt less at their mercy.

I was relieved when the supervisor for my creative research project turned out to be a varsity mate from the earlier years. I had seen too many personality clashes result in miserable students trying to finish their all-important honours project. However, my relief was short-lived. The varsity mate was pretty hard-arsed and made me feel like the intellectual dwarf of critical thinking. However, I did not give up. I pushed him hard when he was being unreasonable and pushed myself even harder when I caught myself sulking and not making any progress.

My initial proposal literally ended up in the trash. Then I found my voice. Instead of taking the lazy way out, I drove my stand-up comedy to the limit with this project. If comedy thrived on society's dark corners and grey areas, then it could be a channel for demystifying the very taboos that feed oppressive systems. I decided to write a stand-up special based purely on menstruation. The piece would need to challenge, to speak back. It also had to be funny, otherwise it would just be a monologue.

I actually did it. Guys, I wrote an essay on menstruation. If I was not so hungry for success, I would have registered for my masters to further explore this thing. I identified my political position as a black female comedian over the months that I worked on this project. Whether I do it consciously or not, my identity politicises my comedy. This realisation was the most exciting part of going back to school for me. I got to put myself and my chosen career path under a microscope.

It was not without its challenges, though. In no time at all I was over-worked and unravelling at the seams. I was still working full time as a writer and performer, while raising my one-year-old son. Wits had given me the edge, but I had to make sure not to fall off it. My mother was not doing any better, and her ill-health was taking an emotional toll on me. But I really wanted this, so I stayed focused.

In the end I passed with decent grades, and when my letter of gradu-ation arrived, I took it to Mama with the delight of a schoolkid. Her first graduate. Normally she would not have missed my graduation ceremony for the world, but by the time it occurred in 2011, she had already been hospitalised. She had been looking forward to this day ever since I told her I had finally completed the damn thing, and I could tell that she was heartbroken to miss it. Her health had deteriorated to the point where I was begging God to at least let her see me do this one thing, so I was very emotional at the ceremony. My usual chattiness was gone. Graduating just did not carry the same meaning without my mother there. I fought back tears when my name was called, and I walked across that stage with-out hearing my mother cheer me on.

4

'n Boer maak 'n plan

(*A farmer makes a plan*)

My mother was a firm believer in there being a solution to every problem. You keep moving forward no matter what. She would always say, *''n Boer maak 'n plan'* – a farmer makes a plan. No situation was hopeless until you ran out of ideas. In 2003, I had to put that saying into practice when I got kicked out of Wits for being unable to pay my tuition. But I could not give up, and Mpho was an eternal optimist of a boyfriend who would not *let* me give up. I stayed in Johannesburg and began to hustle. I didn't even know I had it in me to hustle, but I knew that if I went back to Thaba Nchu, I would end up working at Shoprite with three children by four dads (yes, you read that correctly).

I wanted more for myself, and I could not shake the feeling that there was something bigger waiting for me. I would have conversations with God and tell Him that He had got me started on this journey and would need to keep that torch on for me, because the darkness was shaking me up a little. I also felt like I owed Mama a victory. She had made herself sick trying to get me to where I was, stressing over getting me through school and this far at university, so I was not about to be anything less than what she had imagined for me: successful. I also had a younger sister who needed support, and the least I could do for Mama was lighten that load.

Although I wasn't officially enrolled, I went back to the university anyway to be cast in plays that weren't restricted to students – plays directed

45

by seniors or staff. I needed an agent to see me in action, and I needed the work. I was cast in *Quarter Life Crisis* by a senior student, and the play was privately funded to be staged at the Grahamstown National Arts Festival. After a successful showing at Grahamstown, the play had its first run at Wits University, and a few agents were invited. This was a very important show for me. I needed to make an impression.

Of all the agents I had heard of, Penny Charteris and Moonyeen Lee were on top of my wish list. They represented the top actors across all the disciplines, from film and television to theatre. I wanted in. Badly. Penny was already Mpho's agent and, although he wouldn't admit it, I think he put in a good word for me. Penny honoured an invite to one of my performances at the Downstairs Theatre at Wits. We met after the show and had what felt like an awkward conversation. I introduced myself as Relopile Morake, and her response was, 'Well, nobody is going to remember that name. Do you have a shorter version?'

I said, 'Everyone calls me Tumi,' and Tumi Morake was born. Penny told me, right there outside the Downstairs Theatre, to henceforth introduce myself by that name. Rolls off the tongue, easy to remember.

She invited me to visit her office in Parkhurst later in the week. I was elated. Mpho drove me there a couple of days later. Penny was a no-nonsense type of agent. She asked you what you wanted, and then told you what she expected and could do for you. I was honest with her about my financial situation, but she kept me on nevertheless, on the understanding that I would focus on paying back the university and finishing my degree.

Now, I do not have the archetypal look for any character, so getting auditions was hard, and getting call-backs even harder. I was not thin enough to be the hot lead and I was not plump enough to be the fat friend. My accent was the ugly stepchild of Afrikaans, Setswana and government-school English. The cockroach maintained her confidence, however; this could be a unique selling point, not a deterrent.

I soon hit another hurdle, though. Being in a play meant attending rehearsals, but I was in plays with students, so rehearsals happened after hours. I lived in Protea Glen, Soweto – two taxi rides away, and the nearest taxi rank was on the other side of town. I began asking my friends for help, and it came so easily it humbled me. Half the time I never even had to ask. I would bump into someone who would want to know why they did not see me on campus any more, and I would tell them, matter-of-factly, about my financial exclusion and my intention to make it back in. Each time I would be offered temporary accommodation. So I began squatting on campus with people who would share not only their lodgings, but also their food with me. Sometimes they would even gift me money I had not asked for. Shuki, a friend I had made in first year, insisted that I stay with her for a bit. As usual, though, there was a snitch, and a newsletter went out threatening students who were harbouring squatters with expulsion from residences and disciplinary action from the university.

I figured that while *Quarter Life Crisis* was on at Wits, I could sneak back after the show and sleep in the green room or the changing rooms. Lucky for me, another acquaintance, who then became my friend for life, somehow found out about my situation and took me in. I was embraced in a way that I can only explain as God sending me real-life angels. Plus, He knows what a weakling I am; I don't think I would last a day on the streets.

All the while, I was attending auditions, bombing and applying for work wherever I could – even waitressing. I would get occasional work as an animal character in those hot fluffy suits, or for marketing companies. I don't remember ever hating those jobs; there were just easy days and tough days. With Sally's Party Services we were working for a woman with a heart of gold, so it was easy. We would go to shopping malls dressed like dragons. We got to play for six hours and get paid for it. I loved it.

The tough came with super-rich brats who would abuse you while you were wrapped in a walking sauna. We did some family event in the sum-mer just before the December holidays, and this little blonde girl kept attacking me. She looked like the anti-Christ's second cousin: beautiful, no front teeth and buzzing on a sugar high. She was pulling me violently, pushing and kicking me, and not letting me play with the other kids. I bent down, put on a scary voice and told her that I turned evil when I got mad. I did not see her again after that.

The direct-marketing gigs were also okay. At some point, I was mar-keting toilet paper in supermarkets, and my sense of humour had to come to my rescue. It was my job to find creative ways of convincing people that their bums preferred the more expensive three-ply toilet paper to the usual two-ply. Having to bother people who are minding their own business, doing their shopping, and then getting them to spend more money than they intended to, sets you up for all sorts of nonsense. It was a shitty job – okay, you saw that one coming – but I learnt a lot about parking my ego and my pride to get what needed doing done.

My money was spent on travelling to and from gigs or workshops, and contributing to the kitty of whoever was giving me a place to sleep. This eased the financial pressure on my mother, as I didn't have to keep calling home for funds. I felt my younger sister needed the financial support more than I did. Also, I worried that my mother would get herself into more debt if she thought I was cash-strapped in Johannesburg. I stressed enough about her mental well-being, so I wanted to be the last thing she worried about.

When I could, I attended free scriptwriting and creative workshops run by the SABC and independent bodies. I was determined to get into the TV industry one way or another, and upskilling made the most sense. Whatever I was missing out on at Wits, I was sure I could get directly from the industry. And, eventually, it paid off. It was at a workshop that I met Akin Omotoso and Makhaola Ndebele, who would later give me my first TV writing gig. That gig led to *Izoso Connexion*, which got me my first lead TV gig and a gig on a soapie, and so on.

Why am I sharing this with you? Because people see you doing well and assume that you are lucky, that you are getting jobs willy-nilly because you know so and so. Or they ask, why you and not them? Who are *you* to be landing these gigs? Well, my hustle has been constant and focused and I am where I am because I busted my ass and held on like a bull terrier. I stayed hungry, showed up and delivered. Often, I have heard people say, 'You are everywhere; open up the industry.' I just think, *I worked so hard to kick those doors down, so how about maybe you find yourself a gap?*

But before all those doors opened, Mpho's father heard about my predicament and gave me a job as a telemarketer for his insurance franchise. I revelled in that one, too. I would put on different voices and really play at getting those appointments. When telemarketers call me, I am probably a little kinder than most people, because I picture the former Tumi with a lame script in front of her and a target for the day. It can break your soul, especially if it's a job you *have* to do, not one you *want* to do.

My days became predictable and I lost a lot of weight. Life was losing its lustre, and I needed to get it back. To my great relief, I finally landed an acting gig, with Arepp Theatre for Life, spreading awareness about abuse, bullying, hygiene and other youth issues via plays and puppetry. We would train the teachers to use the material provided by Arepp to reinforce the stuff we covered in our performances. When Arepp confirmed that I would be joining them, it was like getting a new lease on life. As an educational theatre company, it toured the country with performances tailor-made for different age groups. I would be able to work on my acting *and* change lives. It was awesome. I quit my telemarketing job the very next day, even though the gig would only start about two months later.

With Arepp I finally started making a decent living, which allowed me to save up for Wits, pay my rent and send something home. I paid *mashori*, which is when you give your very first salary to your uncles or buy them something with that money (the pay from the telemarketing job didn't count; it didn't stretch beyond my basic needs). I took the easy way out, with beer and cigarettes. My new job meant I had to get a tax number, because my salary was actually high enough now to fall into a tax-paying bracket. I bought my first pair of Ray-Bans and got my first phone contract. I felt like I was officially adulting.

I enjoyed my work at Arepp. It offered me a chance to change people's lives or affect them positively while doing something I loved. I got to travel the country, and even go home for free, because we would end up in that area when touring the Free State. It was also a great way to learn new skills and work with trained actors from other institutions.

Arepp also landed me in therapy, and I mean this in a good sense. I was not quite in touch with what was happening with me psychologically and emotionally. The nature of the work at Arepp meant you had to have the skill set to debrief after your experiences, but it wasn't helping. Dealing with issues of abuse in our work often meant that we would be the first people to whom these kids would report abuse. The disclosures became too much for me. We would also get hit on by teachers and high-school students, and a couple of times I had to stop myself from punching people in the throat. I started suffering from anxiety attacks and seemed to be falling into a depression. It did not help that, at home, Mama could not get a handle on her bipolar disorder.

My boss put me in touch with a counsellor at LifeLine. I began unpacking so much pain that I would have massive headaches after our sessions. But the therapy helped me with my temper too. God has this thing where He doesn't quite give you what you want but a means to get there, which then turns out to be exactly what you needed. I never imagined that Arepp would be more than just a financial breakthrough for me, but the vehicle that would lead me to finally finding a way of unpacking the trauma in my own life.

I would be away with Arepp for entire school terms at a time, and be home over the school holidays. When we were in Johannesburg, I would go to the SABC to attend writing and creative TV workshops, because I still wanted to be on the commercial side of the industry. I kept my eye on the ball. In my time at Arepp, I was directed by Krijay Govender, another excellent female comedian whose directing skills have since taken the TV industry by storm. She told me to try out stand-up comedy. I told her that I had, and she insisted that I find myself an agent who could get me noticed on that scene. I had no idea that there were agents in comedy. Penny Charteris certainly wasn't a stand-up-comedy agent, plus the industry was still finding its feet in those days.

In the meantime, Arepp was losing sponsors, and in the middle of our contracts, with six months to go, our jobs ended. I wasn't too worried. I was writing for my first sitcom gig, *Nomzamo*, so my investment in all those workshops was paying off. The pressure now, though, was to replace the monthly salary I was losing with something that could pay the rent, support my sister and still keep me going, too. Mpho and I were separated at this time, to add salt to the wound. He felt I was smothering him, and he had lost interest in me. I was shattered; I loved the hell out of that guy. I knew I was incredibly jealous and possessive, but so was he! My world seemed to be coming a little undone. In retrospect, we each had a little more growing up to do.

I had moved to a bachelor flat in Yeoville that my sister nicknamed Yizo Yizo, after the huge hit drama series about a dysfunctional school in the township, plagued by corrupt teachers, rebellious students and disruptive gangs. I think the location of the flats reminded her of that fictional dystopia. The building looked rough and derelict on the outside and made me look like I was really slumming it in Johannesburg, but inside was one of the oldest and best-kept flats in Yeoville, with well-preserved wooden floors and pressed ceilings. It was an easy walk from town to Yizo Yizo, and I was not afraid of Yeoville or Hillbrow. It was downtown Johannesburg that, in my head, was the devil's playground. These parts were just an extension of West Africa with scatterlings of East. I felt safe in Yeoville, and the worst thing that ever happened to me was an on-the-spot marriage proposal, which I sweetly declined. Hey, man, our brothers from across the border loved my rotund self, shame.

My mother always waited for the title sequence of *Nomzamo* and then called me to tell me that she'd seen my name. I was also writing for *Muvhango*, one of the big TV soapies. I was bitter that I had not been cast in it a couple of years before, when I auditioned, but I really enjoyed writing for it. My family always messaged me to say that they had seen my episodes. They really are the best cheerleaders. It felt good. Mama was convinced that I had made it in life, and expected that my next step would be to write myself into *Muvhango*.

But my dreams were a little bigger than that. In the rare quiet times I had in the flat, when I was waiting for the next round of writing, I realised I had the time to do other things – performing, or even developing my skills. It was time for me to explore the idea that Krijay had put in my head of performing stand-up comedy and putting myself out there. I had no excuse: I had the time, I had the talent. All I needed was the nerve, the agent and the gigs.

I had no idea where to start, so I sought someone out who did. Krijay was more of a Durban baby, so I called Judy-Jake Tsie, the only woman I knew who was a working comedian in Johannesburg. And a good one at that. It was time to bite the bullet. I had a strong ten minutes; all I needed was a stage.

5

My baby, you are a trier

Every time I excelled at something, Mama would say, 'My baby, you are a trier.' It was her way of saying that she was impressed, that I was making waves. I liked that she called it 'trying', because everything I ventured into was a trial. I have never been cocksure; I have just told myself that if I can learn something, I can master it.

Mama and I shared many laughs. She was naughty, and she always made people laugh. My father also has a fantastic sense of humour, and no shortage of dry jokes. Their combined genes created this comedic beast that is Tumi Morake. When I ventured into the entertainment industry, it was with the aim of mastering whichever craft I took a liking to, and I took an extra-special liking to comedy. I now believe comedy is my calling. It is a journey I am still on, forever learning and growing.

I have a firm footing in four arenas of the entertainment industry: stand-up comedy, acting, writing and presenting, probably in that order. My journey into stand-up comedy was rather seamless. Of all the challenges I ever undertook, stand-up comedy was the easiest, probably because it's an industry which, in many ways, is always ahead of its time. During the bad old days of apartheid, comedy got away with calling out P.W. Botha on his nonsense via the character of Evita Bezuidenhout. When stand-up comedy started growing commercially, it was spearheaded by young black comedians such as David Kau, Ashifa Shabba and Kagiso Lediga, to name a few. Then, when women began playing in that space, we were embraced and pushed onto as many platforms as possible, often backed by male comedians. I was a female comedian working nights in dingy clubs, and these guys made me feel safe. I just had to make sure I did not die on stage. Ah, the wonderful language of comedy. Kill or die. You kill, you win; you die, you work on your resurrection and come back stronger.

When I first branched into stand-up comedy, it was because I had finally happened onto something I could approach with the confidence of a cockroach.

The first time I ever did stand-up was for a final-year student who had written a script for three comedians or comic actors. I can tell jokes, I reckoned, so why not? At the audition, there was a queue of boys and only two girls. I was not fazed. I grabbed a script, stepped outside, prepped. I laughed so hard before I even memorised the script that I must have looked like I was sucking up. I could see the other actors trying to figure the gags out.

I remembered the words of my Grade 4 teacher, Mrs Walker, who told me that I had an innate understanding of humour. I got the jokes that went over most of the class's heads. At this audition, I already felt like I had an edge on everyone else. Delivery is *everything* in comedy. I have heard the best gags fall flat simply because the comedian was a better writer than presenter, and let me tell you, honey, the audience is there to be tickled, not to decipher the funny.

When my turn came, I stood in front of this beautiful, tiny Greek girl with long dark hair and a friendly face. I remember the relief I felt when she laughed before I had even begun going through her gags. I was cast with two other guys, and I never looked back. Using the Greek student's structure, I began coming up with my own gags. She had a very Seinfeld-esque narrative technique: that observational style of comedy that unpicks the details of day-to-day living and makes the most mundane things hilarious. I used it to learn how to write my own material.

The first gag I ever wrote was about a prison hunger strike that had made headlines at the time. I said it was only fair that the hunger strikers save us some tax money, since we feed them anyway, and it could even solve the issue of overcrowding in prisons by killing inmates off. I joked that the hunger strike seemed more like a self-correcting mechanism than a problem. Another early gag was about the acoustics in public toilets that made it difficult for anyone to do a number two. I would make the sound of the poop dropping into the water, the echo of that embarrassing broadcast, and the extra-hard, unnecessarily loud coughing fit you use to try to mask the sound. Then sitting in your cubicle until you were sure that the restroom was empty, because you did not want whoever had heard you to see who had made the number two. It was a crappy gag, but I sold it and got that first big laugh that spurred me on to write more.

I grew steadily from there. The first time I performed in a comedy festival was in 2004, when Mpho organised a charity gig for Rotaract in the Downstairs Theatre of Wits University. This was to be the inaugural Best Medicine Comedy Show, benefiting local orphanages. Mpho was assembling a huge comedy line-up at a time when comedy fests were a rare thing. He talked me into doing five minutes, because he was convinced I was hilarious. I was convinced that the guy was just so in love with me that he actually thought I could stand among giants.

An unfamiliar nervousness came over me, but it was also exciting in a way I had never experienced before. Mpho's line-up included his sister Nana Yaa and some established comedians my brave young man had decided to call to get this thing done. He had worked with them on *The Phat Joe Show* and was positive they would be down.

This was how I learnt the simple strategy of 'the worst thing they can do is say no'. Mpho called them up one by one: Riaad Moosa, Joey Rasdien, Kagiso Lediga, Tshepo Mogale and Dale Abrahams. All of them agreed to appear. David Kau played hardball and initially refused, but on the night he showed up and said he'd jump on. It was insane! I tried to chicken out, but my man was having none of it. A couple of other students were also going to jump on for five minutes. We were excited. Sceptical, but excited. Kagiso came up to me backstage and asked me what my star sign was. I told him Sagicorn, and he said, 'You're gonna die.' I wanted to punch him in the throat. Then I realised he was going around to all the new-timers and asking them that question. We all had a laugh, although I faked mine because I was too terrified to find anything funny.

I clutched my little piece of paper with my planned set. I wasn't going to make the five-minute mark, but I would be happy with three. My voice lecturer at the time, Pam Power (prolific writer, friggin' amazing, funny as hell), came to watch and told me afterwards that this was a career path I should definitely consider. She was impressed. This was a sharp-shooter who did not give compliments willy-nilly, so I held onto her words like she had just given me a distinction in performance.

It would take me another three years to jump on stage at a comedy club, but stand-up stayed on my mind during the post-Wits hustle, and eventually became an obsession. I saw it as a platform for fearless speech. That quality, or promise, drew me to the art. The absence of sacred cows in the material promised me a certain level of satisfaction that I would not get from anything else I was involved in as a performer or a writer. My other work imposed limitations set by censorship, or I would find myself diluting my thoughts by expressing them through fictional characters. What I wanted was to join the sacred home of the marginalised, where I could speak freely, against the system, against the status quo, without fear of retribution. The way African American comedians talked back to the dominant ideology and power.

I got in touch with Judy-Jake Tsie, another talented female comedian, to ask her how I could get five minutes on a comedy stage. She had the contacts; I needed the connection. The first one was a gig for Joe Parker in a casino complex called Carnival City. Carnival City is in the East Rand of Johannesburg, in Brakpan. From the outside it looked like a giant, dome-shaped fun park with blue, red and yellow lights. Walking in, I found a giant casino that felt worlds apart from reality. The only other place where I'd heard that much Afrikaans being spoken was in Bloemfontein. I felt right at home.

We walked across the winding walkways and came to the lily-white Supersport Bar, where wafting cigarette smoke hung in the air, mingling with the smell of fermented saaz hops. This was a very male space. Invisible testosterone flexed its muscles here. And because it was the end of the month, the room was packed to capacity. My nerves began kicking in.

We came in through the front, facing the stage. The show preceding ours was still on: a 'tits-and-ass show', as the comics called it. Heavily made-up girls in skimpy costumes and super-high heels; these were the only female performers we encountered in that space. Wonderful. We went to wait in the back because the dressing rooms were occupied by either dancers or dancers' things. I didn't mind; I couldn't sit still anyway. The audience was mainly drunk, mainly white, mainly male. The women who were there were either accompanying those men or were probably on a gambling break. And after the tits-and-ass show, I daresay those men were a tad randy and in the mood for action rather than comedy. The last thing they wanted now, I imagined, were some chancers trying to make them laugh. However, Judy-Jake convinced me that it would be great; I had a strong five minutes, and that was all I needed to sell myself to this room. An open spot is an unpaid spot, but this was my chance to prove I was good enough to be a paid act.

One of the comics told me that this was a tough crowd, but I would do all right if I just got up there, did my time and got off. Well. When I walked on stage, the audience continued to speak among themselves. A couple of comedians had already been bodied, so I was prepared to die. Some people in the audience seemed thrown; I may have been the first black female comedian they had ever seen. I decided to address the elephant in the room by saying that I was wearing too many clothes compared to the last show and that I probably looked out of place. I assured them that my madam had given me the night off to come and do comedy (because, let's face it, they were way more familiar with black women as domestic workers than as witty stand-up comedians). They chuckled, and I noticed that the room had gone quiet. I thought I was dying, but when the first big laugh hit and was followed by silence, I realised these guys were with me. They were buying into my story and waiting for me to keep going. I owned my space.

The next morning I got a call from Joe Parker asking me if I would like to make some money, and that's how I booked my first paid comedy gig. I was ecstatic. What followed was a visit to Comedy Underground, run by the grungiest, darkest, most intelligent comedian I had ever come across: John Vlismas. This, I was told, was the Mecca of Comedy. You could die a horrendous death one Sunday and rule the night the next.

It was called the Underground because, duh, it was underground, in the underbelly of Cool Runnings in Melville, a bar and restaurant whose menu read 'Food takes about 30 minutes, if we can find the chef'. Newcomers thought it was a cute joke; regulars knew it was a fair warning.

Downstairs, beneath the wooden floors and Caribbean ambience that welcomed you to this tropical vibe, was a hot, dimly lit cave. Descending into it felt like going to hell in order to ask the devil for a free pass. It was a real dungeon, but legends were born there.

The Underground had its own bar, and a small stage that seemed carved out of the building. That corner housed the sound guy, the line-up, the night's supply of drinks for the acts, and the host. There was no shortage of recreational drugs and alcohol. My drug of choice was beer, but my respect for performance art meant I would only get my fix after a set.

The audience in that place loved comedy. Melville was the feeding ground for many university students and hippies from Wits, the University of Johannesburg and Wits Tech, and they were young, open-minded and hungry for a different kind of entertainment. It would get so packed that you could not walk without making physical contact with someone. There would be people standing against the wall to watch. The atmosphere was electric, and Comedy Underground became a cult for me.

John was the high priest, we were his clergymen, and the audience were insatiable followers caught in this trance of mirth and maniacal laughter. There were comedians who were stars only in the dungeon. The world above was not ready for them, but down there, they were legends. Most of the time it would get so full that the acts would have to climb over eager, queuing crowds just to get to the back of the stage. The backstage area was literally in the men's room, and even the girls chilled in there. Guys would come in and do their business, and you'd be chatting casually with other comics like it was just another day at the office.

When I say comedy has always been ahead of its time, I mean it. No girl ever felt threatened in that space (at least not that I know of). We were all comedians, and we were all there to be thrown into the pit to either come out dead or with a big kill. I *loved* it. It made of me a kind of beast I otherwise could not have become. My fear died there. You were prepared to die on that stage, if needs be, because it made resurrection that much sweeter. It was your training ground for whatever next-level step you were about to take – festivals, corporates, one-man shows. If you were bad at keeping to your time, ice would be thrown at you; you learnt quickly. If you sucked, the hosts were merciless. This was the comedy dojo, and I miss it with all my heart.

We would get paid as if we had just sold some illicit drugs – a discreet handshake left a fee in your palm, and that was that. I never cared how much I got paid – I just cared that I got to be on stage and lived.

Then something happened which would seriously affect my decision to pursue a career in comedy. It was one of the turning points for me: I heard John Vlismas being interviewed on radio. He was my comedy hero, so I turned up the volume. John was punting a show he was doing, and the deejay asked him which hot new acts to look out for. When he said my name – Tumi Morake, name and surname – I was so proud. I had no idea that the man had even committed my name to memory, and here I was, hearing it on the radio for the first time in my life – from a legend saying I was destined for greatness. I decided I would prove him right. I had no choice; he had already told the world I was coming, so my ass had to get into gear and deliver. The cockroach confidence was suddenly stronger than ever.

There were only three dedicated comedy clubs in Johannesburg when I was starting out. Each of those places was a minimum of two taxi rides away from my base. Underground was the easiest to get to, and a cab there was not too expensive. The other two places, though, were a whole other story. Carnival City, in Brakpan, was on the other side of town for me, and Morula Casino in Mabopane was a gig I did purely for the money and the practice, not for the love. The audience was ungovernable, and there was always a random comedian who turned his ten minutes into a forty-minute one-man show. And it was an hour away from where I lived. I needed wheels, badly.

Mpho would drive me when he was available, but he lived with his parents and would have to borrow his dad's car. It was a lot of admin for him. Considering South Africa's infamous reputation for violence against women, the idea of finding my way around Johannesburg and surrounds at night, using public transport, was not an attractive one. One or two comics were always willing to help out with a ride, but I hardly knew some of them. I made many an awkward phone call asking for a lift from guys who had never even met me before. It was a logistical nightmare, especially because they came from all over Johannesburg.

Three experiences eventually forced me to go out and buy a car – before I even had a driver's licence. The first was with a comedian who, bless his heart, received a call from his dealer on our way home, and detoured to pick up his coke before dropping me off. We had left the gig late because he'd been socialising, and, hey, he was my ride, so I was at his mercy. It was approaching midnight when we eventually left the gig and that call came in. Now, I'm a small-town girl. I do not know what people are like on cocaine, and I have watched a lot of American cop dramas where undercover cops pretend to be dealers so that they can nab people buying drugs. I was dressed well, made up, and driving with a white man in the middle of the night. All I could think of was what would happen if the cops caught this guy with drugs and a young black woman sitting in his car. I would be arrested for possession of drugs and prostitution. This guy and I did not gel like friends, I had only ever done a couple of gigs with him, and I knew nothing about him but his name and surname, yet here I was, riding around Joburg with him after midnight. It was the longest ride of my life.

In the second incident, I was in the car with people who had been smoking weed and drinking. It was mid-winter in Johannesburg, the degrees sitting in negative integers, and these guys were driving with the windows open. *Even* on the highway, at high speed. I was convinced my ears had frostbite and my bones were trying to separate themselves from my flesh. I actually had tears in my eyes. Was I really this desperate to do comedy?

The final nail in the coffin was getting a lift with a comedian who was late and drove like a complete maniac. Judy-Jake Tsie and I were in the car, and this guy was driving so fast we stopped talking and started praying. Then his car cut out in the middle of the highway and started slowing down by itself. Divine intervention. By chance, a fellow comedian was on the same highway and took us home while this guy sorted out his car.

The very next day I applied to write my learner's test. In the meantime, I had landed myself a nice TV role that would pay me a decent amount. I was already receiving a writing salary, so I decided not to touch the acting money. I asked my agent to only pay me at the end of the entire shoot so that I could use that money to buy a car.

Three months down the line, my friend put his car up for sale and I jumped at the opportunity. Twenty thousand rand bought me my freedom in the form of a light-blue 1990 Toyota Corolla. This car had killer sound – loud enough to start its own street bash and the kind of bass that reverberated in your chest.

I called it Tyte. When I bought it, I was still one of those learner drivers who stalled practically every time I had to change gears at a stop sign. I once stalled on an incline and began to panic because there was traffic around and I loathe being hooted at. Give me the middle finger, but don't make your car scream at me. Anyway, the car behind me had been waiting and I was going into a panic because I kept stalling and was trying not to roll back. Eventually, the gentleman behind me simply drove around. As he passed, he rolled down his window and I braced myself for an onslaught of verbal abuse. What followed stayed with me forever. He gave a gentle toot of the horn, and when I looked at him, I was met with a smiling face. 'Take your time, you'll get it!' he said. My cousin and I laughed, and she said I should call my car that – Take Your Time. So I went with the acronym, and it stuck.

A few months after buying Tyte, I drove, solo, to my dad's place, four hours away. It was an emotional trip. I thought about how I had gone from taking the train to taking a taxi to taking a bus, and now I was driving myself home. As usual, the waterworks started. I took my time.

I loved that car. I learnt so much from it – how to change a tyre, how to know when the fan belt was an issue, the magic of antifreeze, the joys of filling up with nitrogen. When I sold Tyte, I cried. It had been one of the highlights of adulting for me. My first car. Failing a driver's test twice and getting it on the third attempt. Like that guy said, I should take my time. Failing sucked, but I jumped back in as soon as I could and queued for a new date right after having had a cry in the bathroom. I knew I would lose my nerve if I gave up.

My father suggested that I get tested in Bloemfontein – smaller city and a better car, because I would use his. I completed that test with five minutes remaining. I knew I had done nothing wrong, but the man testing me was so mean, I was convinced he was going to fail me. When we were finished, he handed me a piece of paper. Tears welled up in my eyes. Only then did he realise he was dealing with a human being, and said, 'Go back inside to queue for your licence.' I could have hugged him. But he was so surly, I decided against it.

In July 2009, four months after the birth of my son Bonsu, I performed in my first Vodacom Comedy Festival, the most lucrative gig of my comedy career at the time. The festival was run by Eddy Cassar, a man I called the comedy gangster. He had this Italian Mafia vibe about him. A warm man with a perfect tan, well dressed, and very Catholic. All his phone calls ended with 'God bless'. We had a little fallout in the middle of the run when he told me that I didn't need the word 'pussy' in my comedy. It was a lazy gag about Women's Month that played on the theme song for the Yellow Pages: 'Let your fingers do the walking through the yellow pages.'

Twenty thousand women marched to the Union Buildings to protest pass laws in 1956. That means, for one whole day, twenty thousand men got no food and no sex. Sure, I can understand the food, but sex? We deserve a theme song for Women's Day: 'Let your pussy do the walking to Parliament.' It *always* got a laugh, but Eddy seemed to take issue with it. I didn't mind and would happily have scrapped it, but he brought it up at the dinner table, embarrassing me in front of fellow comics and invited guests. Two things I do not cope well with are being told what to do, and public humiliation. It would be another six years before I worked with Eddy again. Yep, I am *that* sensitive.

That said, that Vodacom Comedy Festival turned out to be the best gig for my career. I got called to Cape Town by different companies for comedy appearances, I received lovely media coverage, and I was even given a bad but useful review that mentioned my name and helped me to improve my set. The critic remembered me; that counted for something. My love for comedy was cemented and my hunger to thrive in the industry was fuelled. I reworked my set, made it less disjointed, and by the time I left the festival, I had found my comedy rhythm. Tumi Morake had developed a persona. I took to the stage to kill and take no prisoners.

I was ready to make comedy my bitch.

6

You are too free

One of Mama's fears was that I would never get married. She would say, 'Boitumelo, you are too free, you will scare men away.' It was as if she both admired and disliked my independence. I used to tell her that I could give her the grandchildren she wanted, but I couldn't guarantee that I'd be married to their father. I couldn't understand how Mama had managed to raise me all by herself for the better part of my life, but was so insistent that I be married before having children. She was a return soldier herself (divorced), so why did she want me to conform?

This was one of the few ways Mama disappointed me. She could be so worldly yet so old school, like the time she got upset with me at my uncle's funeral. Mpho and I were dating, and Mama was telling an aunty how I would be marrying Mpho and bringing lots of grandkids. I told her she was right about the grandkids, but that I was not keeping the pig just for the bacon.

She literally stopped speaking to me for the rest of the afternoon.

My parents' divorce had made me question marriage and what the point of it was. My parents were quite similar in personality, and in many ways they had married themselves. I figured, if people who seemed like such a perfect match could come to detest each other so much, what about people who are completely different? How could you sustain a marriage if you are pulling in opposite directions? My turnaround came from observing Mpho's parents. They give each other enough space to be who they are, and somehow it works. I also realised that Mpho and I differ in a complementary way. We make up for each other's weaknesses, and we back each other's strengths.

But back to my parents. Those two were so in love when they were still together. Always cosy, always joking and enjoying each other's company when they were at home. At least, that was my experience of them. I only remember one major fight from when they were together. But how things changed when they finalised their divorce, though. They truly could not stand each other. However, Mama never said anything bad to me about my father. Maybe with everyone else she told it like it was, but to me, she always found diplomatic ways of dealing with him. She did not ask for child support, she did not sue for child support, she just did what she could. Of course she won full custody when she divorced my dad, as he was in jail. I don't think anything else would have made sense. I am quite grateful that fate placed me in her care. As a woman living in a world that is not very kind to women, it was important that I grow up watching a fighter in action. A pioneer who inspired me to stand strong and make things happen for myself.

But Mama created a monster without even realising it. She was such a fighter that I inevitably found myself learning to be battle-ready. Now, when I say 'battle', I do not mean 'confrontation'. I mean ready to take on the world, to refuse to give in to adversity and to be boxed to suit people's perceptions. Conflict is a different kind of battle. I hate it, because I am afraid of unintentionally hurting people with my words. I am also afraid of how far my temper can push me. I once got very angry and frustrated with my mother after I found her with some marijuana. She had been skipping out on her medication, so I was already worried sick about her. Finding the marijuana pushed me over the edge. I physically attacked her when she swore at me, after I had calmly asked her why she was making her situation worse. She had gone missing for a week before this incident.

I had never seen her with the stuff before, and I never saw her with it again. It must have been something she happened upon when she was on one of her manic highs. I am so ashamed and sad that I attacked her. Fortunately, my uncle stopped the altercation. I sobbed uncontrollably – I didn't know what had come over me, I just knew I was hurting deeply.

Everyone had predicted that she was going to fail in trying to raise me and Vonani by herself, but she was fiercely determined to prove that she could do it. And she did.

So why she took such issue with me wanting to be independent, I do not know. I saw her as the poster mom for single-parenting, and I found it empowering. I did not feel the need to be bound to the usual strategy of marrying the man to have the babies. I could still be with this man as a choice we both make every day, and just raise some people either separately or together. I had seen that it could work, not just through my mother, but through her younger sister and some of my mother's single-parent friends. It really did not seem like a big deal.

Of course, I was also convinced that no man would ever marry me – not even Mpho. I was just not … domesticated enough. I suppose, in many ways, and much like me, Mama had done things out of either necessity or desire, not because she was consciously trying to change the world. But I wanted to navigate this space of child-rearing and relationships like a modern woman who has options. The concept of women *needing* men was foreign to me.

I mean, come on, even Disney was producing kiddies' movies made up of single-parent families; the world was moving forward. Nevertheless, Mama was in many ways a pioneer: she was well-read, she loved medicine and she loved people. A lot of people have said she should have been a doctor. I disagree. Mama's love for interacting with people would not have been fulfilled as a doctor.

As with my mother, people have their own ideas of what I should be or whom I should be with, but I always choose the path that lights up my spirit. I had spent so much time with guys as a youngster that I never knew what kind of man I wanted to be with romantically. I figured if he liked sport, smelt good most of the time and would share his beer with me, he qualified as my ideal man.

A friend of mine once said I should date older men because I was too much to handle for a guy my own age. I thought she meant in a sexual way, and I was a little taken aback, but she meant I had lived a little too much. I did not have enough patience for a guy in my peer group, and I certainly needed a disciplinarian. Although I dated guys older than me, it wasn't a conscious choice. It just so happened that I clicked better with men who were older than me.

Enter Mpho Osei-Tutu.

If you had told me back then that Mpho would one day be my husband, I would have laughed so hard at you. Here was this black kid, with bongo dreadlocks and an accent that misled you as to its origin. He had attended English-medium schools his whole life and spent most of his school career studying and living in the East Rand. He looked like an identity crisis waiting to happen, *and* he was nine days younger than me.

I was not interested – or so I thought. At university, I gave him a hard time for being a teacher's pet who got away with not working half as hard as us on accruing credits, because he was cast in all the big plays. Initially he annoyed me, but his gentle nature won me over and we eventually became good friends. When he started working for an events company, he hooked me up with a clowning gig. He must have thought he was helping me score some pocket money, but it was a real lifeline for me. Even my then boyfriend thought Mpho was a real sweetheart.

So Mpho became the best man I had ever met. We became friends because he was such a humble, cool soul. He was so comfortable in his manhood, and to this day I have never seen him display any machismo. He is a man, and he doesn't need to prove it. That made me feel incredibly comfortable with him. In fact, I hadn't felt that comfortable with a man since Maestro. I instinctively knew that I was safe with Mpho.

By our third year at Wits, Mpho and I had grown very close. We started officially dating in early 2002. About six months into our relationship, he decided it was time for me to meet his parents. I had met his dad in passing when we were still clowning for Sally, but when I met him as Mpho's girlfriend, he gave me the third degree as if he had never seen me before. He asked me who I was, where I was from, how I had met Mpho, where I lived in Johannesburg, what my parents did for a living – all in one sitting. Mpho got very upset that I was being grilled like this, and I was mortified.

In contrast, his mother Mme and I hit it off instantly. She was warm, and we shared a love for solving puzzles. She had also lived and worked in Thaba Nchu, like my mother – at the same hospital, even. So we had a starting point. We would spend hours on code-word and cryptic puzzles.

I felt so at home. I had already met Mpho's sister, who was also lovely. Both Mme and Nana Yaa would look you in the eye, smile from the heart and make you feel like you were the most interesting person in the world.

Nana Yaa invited me to move in with her about a year into my relationship with Mpho. She lived alone in a huge flat and I needed a place to stay in the city. It would be three years before I moved out, for practical reasons. Living with Nana Yaa is something I will treasure forever. She introduced me to so many things that have stuck with me to this day – among them my love for red wine, Bollywood movies and sci-fi novels. I think of her every time I treat myself to double-cream Ayrshire yoghurt. I had always steered clear of anything that was not low fat, but this delicacy became our guilty indulgence. We would commit and recommit to tae-bo together. I remember the day I broke one of her bowls and ran off to the shops to replace it. By the time I told her what I had done, I was giving her the replacement. She hugged me. She was touched that I cared enough about her and respected her so much that I would do that. I thought it was only right that I replace what I had broken, but she treated this gesture as if I were a good person for doing it. That was part of her magic. She made everyone feel a notch above whatever they felt about themselves. If you needed a sincere cheerleader, Nana Yaa was the best person for the job. She really fed my self-esteem. I admired her, and told her so. Although she was highly intelligent, she played it down.

Nana Yaa kicked serious ass at mathematics, but in her opinion anyone could, they just had to stop being afraid of it. She became fluent in Hindi and was teaching herself animation. Nana Yaa also made the most comfortable, beautiful bras. She was pretty much a dream sister-in-law, and a dream sister in general.

Oh, you should have heard her laugh. To this day, her laughter rings in my ears when I think of her.

When my mother met Mpho, she instantly fell in love with him. She asked me to be gentle with him, because he was such a gentle human. Mama loved his humility and respectfulness. She even told me that he was 'the one'. Look, my mom had called it with all my adult relationships. I had the shortest holiday fling just after high school, and my mother told me we were too excited about each other, that the flame was going to die out as quickly as it had started. Yup, I went to Wits and never looked back. Then the guy before Mpho, she figured he'd have a roving eye. He did. So when she said Mpho was the one, I bought it.

Mpho and I broke up briefly in the third year of our relationship. My friendship with his sister remained intact and life carried on as normal; Nana Yaa and I just didn't talk about her brother. My mother was another story. I told her she had been wrong about Mpho being my future husband. Without batting an eyelid, Mama said that it was just a break and that we were going to end up back together. Yup, she called it – Mpho and I got back together a few weeks later.

I wonder if she saw Mpho as a sort of Messiah for me, someone who would be gentle with me despite how rough I could be. In the last few months of her life, she told me that she'd had a dream in which Mpho had appeared to her as an angel, to take her to heaven in a white car. She thought really highly of my Mpho. She would probably haunt the hell out of me if I let our marriage end. Our marriage certainly has had its challenges, and I have quiet conversations with Mama in which I sense that she is telling me to stop being a pain and just make it work.

Mpho and I have some kind of Midas touch when we work together. We discovered this gift when we were studying at uni. We helped improve each other's marks, and had an electric scene as Feste and Malvolio in *Twelfth Night*. After we left school, we shot a public service announcement on a whim and won an award for the concept. We also realised that we loved similar things about television and theatre, even though our strengths in those fields are quite different. And we riff well together when it comes to conceptualising and creating stories. Mpho, though, is stronger at structuring them. In fact, when we joined forces in our production company, we realised that I was great at selling and he was a great closer.

In 2014, we won a pitch to create a sitcom around a concept we had come up with randomly while riffing about the kind of sitcoms we never get to see on South African television. I loved *Two and a Half Men,* and we agreed that we hadn't seen men raise families on their own in local sitcoms. In fact, I figured it was time to see guys as nurturers and responsible members of society. Thus *Kota Life Crisis* was born: two young brothers raising their younger half-sibling together after their father passes away, leaving them his *kota* business. A *kota* is a township delicacy made up of a quarter loaf of bread, cheese, chips, polony, atchaar and sometimes tomato sauce.

The title is, of course, a play on the term 'quarter-life crisis', when you are in your mid- to late twenties and realise you need to get your act together. We wanted a clever show, one we ourselves would want to watch. The show ran for two seasons, and each one was nominated for awards at the South African Film and Television Awards. Money can't buy that kind of validation.

As Mpho and I have grown in our relationship, we are more and more interlinked in our careers. We are each other's acting coach, sounding board, manager, PA and cheerleader. Neither of us are fans of admin, but Mpho is damn good at it. We also keep each other tied to the family. Our careers get crazy, and at different times we reel each other back in. I have become the convener of family get-togethers and holidays. We each have a vision of creating work of which we can be proud, regardless of the scale at which it is presented or received. We are not chasing fame; we are creating a legacy.

Mpho and I have been together on and off since 2002. In that time, I realised I had hooked up with the kind of guy I couldn't just date on autopilot. He was different – I could never predict his responses to any situation – and that made him all the more attractive to me. He was also very real, very honest.

When the UK band Jamiroquai was in the country, we were so amped about it. I did not have the money for a ticket, but Mpho did, and he went without me. Initially I was mad, but the reality was that we were both students, and I could not justify being mad at him for not giving up an opportunity I would have jumped at too. When he could, he would pay for stuff, but generally we shared the bill. It made me feel like he got my vibe. What I did get every once in a while were flowers and nougat.

Mpho was constantly surrounded by women, but not in a Casanova context. Like me, he just clicked better with the opposite sex. I got it. Unfortunately for him, while we were at Wits, my male friends were the boisterous guys I had met while I was still with Mike.

It took a bit of adjusting, but Mpho and I seemed to balance each other out. He is a kind soul, and I hated seeing anyone take advantage of him. For example, someone would ask him for a lift, then bring three friends without asking him if it was okay, and none of them would offer to help pay for petrol. I would see the frustration on his face but he would still oblige. Since then I've told him to put his foot down, and he has become less and less of a pushover.

I, on the other hand, was not very trusting of people, and Mpho taught me to see the best in people, and to stop looking out for the worst. We also shared a love for soccer, movies and beer. Where we differed was that he loved a plan and I loved spontaneity. Regardless, Mpho and I were excited about each other. We recognised each other's brilliance and encouraged one another a lot. I was not used to that in a relationship. We also shared our dreams with each other, something I had never done with anyone else either.

Because we were both still growing up and finding ourselves, there were times when we needed to be apart – or when we were unsure whether our relationship should be romantic. We would break up amicably and remain friends – this happened in 2004, 2005 and 2008. Eventually, though, we realised that even though we had considered being with other people, we preferred to be with each other. We might not necessarily need each other, but we certainly figured that life would be a little bleak if we weren't together.

In 2008, we decided to get married. Let me rephrase that: Mpho proposed on a whim. He woke up one Easter weekend and decided he really wanted to marry me. So off he went to various jewellery stores, and eventually found a ring that looked exactly like the costume ring I was wearing. I was in Cape Town, but travelling back the next day. He proposed when I got back to Johannesburg.

My mother was ecstatic when she found out. She shouted hallelujah. It warmed the cockles of my heart to see her so genuinely happy for me. I was not following through with the single-affluent-mom plan she had so disliked, and she was getting the son-in-law she wanted. Within two months Mpho had made arrangements for his uncles to meet with my uncles in Bloemfontein, for *magadi* (dowry) negotiations. He jokes that he got me at such a great price, it was like a Black Friday sale.

It took two trips to pay up my *magadi*. After the second trip, a sheep was slaughtered, and we celebrated. Within that month, the Morake delegation travelled with me to Johannesburg to hand me over to my in-laws and exchange gifts, and a new daughter-in-law was welcomed into the Osei-Tutu fold.

Mpho and I were now married under South African customary law, and in the eyes of our family, community and ancestors, but Mpho was a Catholic, so our union had to be blessed for it to bear God's stamp of approval. Until then, many still considered us merely engaged. We were planning to have a white wedding that year so as not to drag the 'engagement' out, and had started going to premarital counselling. It was the first time we actually talked about what we expected marriage to be and how we would raise our kids.

This was stuff we had never actually considered before Father Mike brought it up, and we called the white wedding off because we had too much baggage from the times we had broken up without addressing our reasons for doing so. Then we got back on the wedding train, but discovered we were pregnant shortly before Mpho made the second *magadi* payment, and we postponed the white wedding again. (My uncle still side-eyes me about that; he is convinced that we were hiding the pregnancy at the first *magadi* negotiation, thereby cheating the family out of an extra cow or two.)

I did not want it to look like we were having a shotgun wedding, or to walk down the aisle looking like a giant meringue. Mpho was so freaked out about being pregnant: this was not the plan. We were only supposed to start a family a year or two into the marriage. We rescheduled the wedding for the following year.

A few months after Bonsu's birth, we travelled to Ghana, where we were to be introduced to the greater Osei-Tutu family. Our son would be the first great-grandchild for Mpho's grandmother, and thus marked the start of a new generation of Osei-Tutus.

I had been warned of the heat, but I did not expect the humidity. Nevertheless, I felt like I was on the set of a movie: I had never been surrounded by so much beautiful ebony skin, not even in Yeoville. A huge sign at the airport read 'Akwaaba, Welcome'. And welcome was exactly how I felt.

Visiting Ghana for the first time was a humbling experience. I was in a whole new culinary world. Organic food was the norm, not the exception. I watched *fufu* being pounded, fish being dried. Takeaway food was neither American nor swimming in oil. I was greeted warmly everywhere I went, although I must have looked out of place, because they seemed to know I was a foreigner without me announcing it. I was a foreigner on African soil – that was a first.

I met many well-travelled Ghanaians on that visit. I learnt about how they had given the Queen of England the middle finger at some point in their history, when she wanted to take the Golden Stool, Ghana's royal throne. I learnt that these gentle folk were a very proud people. I also discovered that I had married into a family run by powerful matriarchs, with whom I would have to learn to stand toe to toe. I was hugely intimidated by them. Well-educated, well-travelled, all accomplished in their fields. I could not be ordinary among this extraordinary lot.

I slowly acclimatised to the sweltering, humid heat of Ghana, and my tongue took no time at all getting used to their spicy cooking. It felt like such a different way of life to what I was used to, with a lot of church time, beyond just the usual Sunday vibe. I think there was church three times in the week I was there. Everyone in the family went. The women always looked well put together, and I felt self-conscious in my jeans and shirts. I was also breastfeeding and doing mommy things among these gorgeous women in their beautiful dresses, none with a hair out of place.

What struck me was the love they emanated. They received me with open arms. They probably thought I was struggling with motherhood and I had let myself go, so the next time I travelled there I made a concerted effort to pack nicer clothing and have better hair.

I was fascinated by how well-travelled Mpho's family was. I bonded with his cousins and we talked a lot about the impending wedding. Mpho's aunt, who was due in Indonesia soon, offered to bring back wedding favours. I was gifted some material to make dresses with when I got home.

The reality of the impending big day hit, and excitement began to mount. I knew that everyone was happy and behind us all the way. I was touched by how most of the family had promised to attend our wedding, and delivered on that promise. A week before the ceremony in the Free

State, everyone had arrived, ready to lend a hand, bless us with prayer and party hard.

Mpho and I were real wheelers and dealers with our wedding. I was like a B-list celebrity – at the time, I was writing for *Nomzamo*, a flagship sitcom, I had acted in one season of *Izoso Connexion* and had featured in a film. I was also a regular on South Africa's biggest comedy line-up at the time, *Blacks Only*. Mpho was one of the directors of a major South African drama, *Zone 14*, and was making headway in his acting career. We milked the heck out of that little bit of star power and roped some sponsors into helping us lower the cost of our wedding.

We got *DRUM* magazine on board and decided, to hell with a wedding photographer, we'll negotiate with the magazine's photographer. Eddie was so unobtrusive, it was like there was no press present. We got Converse to sponsor our wedding shoes. I was healing from a staphylococcal infection that would cost me my entire toenail, so high heels were not going to cut it. We also got a huge discount on the cake and decor because of the magazine coverage.

Nana Yaa jumped in at every opportunity to help. I was a little worried about the wedding turning into a big, cheesy event. She was there with magazines and ideas, and came up with the brilliant idea of making eight-month-old Bonsu our ring-bearer. Nana Yaa would wheel him in and we would take the rings from him. It turned out to be one of my favourite parts of the ceremony: her mini jog, pushing the baby in his decorated stroller, while he sat there, pacifier in his mouth, holding a pillow with rings tied to it. Nana Yaa knew how to add that special something to any occasion, and this was one of them.

The biggest spend was on the venue itself, and the food. The guy who owned the place was a sad case – one of those Afrikaans guys who gets sketchy around black people. Up until the wedding we had been dealing with the venue manager, who was smooth and useful.

Then this guy arrived. We had forgotten, up till that point, that we were black people on a private game farm in the Free State. He reminded us. You know when someone is such a stereotype that you begin to think they can't be real? That 'you people' one who keeps a keen eye on the entire event, watching everything like a hawk, as if you could steal his land if he went to the toilet for five seconds? That was him.

We had a great time nonetheless, with me occasionally sneaking off to breastfeed. Bonsu was eight months old and I wanted to breastfeed him until he was two (which I did). The only tragedy of my wedding began and ended in the morning. Father Mike had suggested that we involve our parents more meaningfully in our wedding, to symbolise a coming together of community and family. Mpho and I would both walk down the aisle with our parents accompanying each of us. Mpho would enter with his parents first, then I would follow with mine.

Our parents would then hand us over to each other and embrace each other before we proceeded with the ceremony. My father lost his mind at this suggestion. As I may have failed to mention, he and my mother had major issues. They were civil, but they tried not to be in the same space together for too long. I had also hurt him by not leaving from his house for the chapel, according to our custom.

But I could not have done that to my mother. Heading to the chapel from his home, as opposed to the home I had been raised in by my grandmother, seemed unfair. I wanted to leave from neutral ground, so as not to favour him or my mother, and I decided to leave from the lodge with them.

I did not realise how deeply this had hurt him. On the morning of the wedding, when I was trying to coordinate times with him, he told me that he would not be walking me down the aisle. For all my loudness and outspokenness, I am not confrontational. I am always aware of when I am addressing my elders; it is how I was raised. So I did not argue with my father. I let him say his piece.

Then I tried to explain, but he was not interested. When he had finished, I hung up the phone. Then I collapsed in a heap and cried like a child. I was so hurt. So deeply hurt. My father had let me down before, but this was unforgivable. On a picturesque morning, with springbok roaming, I sat flat on the ground, in my pyjamas, and cried. Solanche, my maid of honour, came running to me. She called for Mpho. They calmed me down and pumped me full of Rescue Remedy. I have no idea how I recovered, but I did. I couldn't even drown my sorrows in drink, because I was still breastfeeding. Rescue Remedy was my best friend.

Despite the family drama, we had a beautiful wedding. My father missed the whole thing, but showed up at the reception, where I spotted him chatting to my in-laws. Before I could say anything, Solanche had already gripped my hand and told me to behave. And I did.

Our wedding was a picture of the wealth of friends Mpho and I had made in our seven-year relationship: Muslim, Jewish, Christian, white, coloured, black, American, Ghanaian, Kenyan, Liberian, Zambian. It probably looked like a meeting of the UN. A reflection of the world Mpho and I lived in, a world where I had been spoilt enough to think I lived in a relatively integrated, progressive society.

So, I had finally bitten the bullet and conformed. I was a kept woman now, and I loved it. I saw marriage not as something I did because society told me to, but because I wanted to be with this guy for the rest of my life, and this was how we wanted it. We would share a last name with our children and would do things as a unit going forward. We were also extending our communities and making them a part of our relationship. They would be witnesses of our commitment to each other; in turn, they pledged allegiance to us as a unit. My mother was so happy. Most importantly, I was so happy.

My relationship with my in-laws continued to grow as we bonded over raising their grandchildren. They are my advisors and support to this very day. When the opportunity came, within a year of our marriage, to join the board of directors in the family business, I felt like I had reached a new level of trust in the family. I look at how much we have achieved as a unit and think how, despite all the challenges I have faced in my life, I have been incredibly blessed. Even when Mpho and I were at our lowest in our marriage, I was supported as a daughter.

Our relationship has suffered blows because I have struggled with the loss of my personal freedom and the obligations that come with the institution of marriage. It is hard enough to face yourself and deal with your own issues, but when you are with someone, it becomes doubly hard. Mostly, our marriage was quite run-of-the-mill, but we went through hell from 2015 to early 2017.

In fact, circa 2016/17, I was sure our marriage was over. I had made my peace with it and I would weather the media storm that would probably follow. Our careers had skyrocketed, but at the same time we were dealing with grief, having lost people very close to us in a short space of time. However, we never slowed down our pace to allow ourselves to grieve properly, or even to simply stop and be in the moment. We kept pushing on, through the pain, through the challenges, and only addressed surface issues; we never delved any deeper. I think we got caught up in the idea of giving each other space. When I reached out, he thought I needed more freedom, and when he reached out, I thought he needed more space.

We found comfort in other people and in our work. It was only a matter of time before it would all come to a head. There was a major lack of intimacy in our relationship, as though we were too broken to allow each other in. When I discovered that Mpho was cheating on me, I kept it to myself. I suffered quietly, and threw myself under an avalanche of work. It was only a matter of time before I, too, found intimacy at work, using the worst excuse – what's good for the goose is good for the gander – to cheat on my husband. It was an escape, a drug that numbed the pain of being so near yet so far away from the man I cared for so deeply.

The beauty of being married to your friend, though, is that you are so open with each other that secrets and sinister corners begin to expose themselves. We caught each other out and then began the arduous task of facing our demons and deciding whether we still wanted this marriage or not. We had let each other down, and the pain was intense and uncomfortable to confront. But we still loved each other deeply, and even our fights, in retrospect, reflected that.

I hadn't realised how much we had lost touch with each other, and with our family and friends. We had become detached from everything that had held us together. I was living like a loner, constantly on the move, and guilt kept me from confiding in my family. The only people I interacted with meaningfully were through work. I began to drift deeper into depression, unaware that this was happening.

It was only when I had a panic attack in the middle of a shoot on the set of *Our Perfect Wedding: She's the One* that I realised I needed help. I thought I was having a heart attack. I felt scared and confused, unable to breathe. Besides shooting *OPW*, I had been dealing with production issues on *Kota Life Crisis* that week and doing corporate events at night. My physician confirmed that I was having a panic attack.

The next day, I was in therapy. Within days, I was on antidepressants. Even though I feel like I lost six months of my life because of those drugs, I also feel like somehow my life was saved. I was saved from myself. I felt nothing over those few months, and with so little emotion I had the capacity to deal with only so much. It was hard on Mpho, who had to figure out how much was the drugs and how much was me just being aloof, but at least I no longer felt overwhelmed.

My mother had always taught me that no matter how bad things get, you step out in your best dress, face made up, head held high. You do not wear your struggles like an advert. I did just that. Being on antidepressants also meant I needed to get fit – I needed to keep moving and eat right. I got a new personal trainer. Mpho and I also attended couple's therapy, and he even began his own therapy. It was a mountain we had to climb.

Our conversations were so heavy, so intentional. It was painful for me to watch him try to lighten up the mood sometimes. It must have been the same for him – I would switch on the Tumi Morake persona, but I did not have the energy to keep it up. I was preoccupied by my own demons. I did not know how to articulate what I felt to my husband, and the frustration built up, but through it all we still prayed together, cried together. We could no longer walk around the pain or find a short cut through it; we had to go through it all and be naked and vulnerable with each other.

In public, we still showed face when we needed to. In 2016, *Kota Life Crisis* had eight nominations at the SAFTAs (South African Film and Television Awards). We arrived separately at the ceremony. Nobody noticed. We posed for some obligatory pictures together and then went home separately. By then our closest friends and colleagues knew that our relationship was in trouble. This was when I learnt who really had my back; some people felt that we should just end it, while others supported us in our fight for our marriage.

Eventually, something clicked into place. I don't know how, or when. But we gradually stopped trying to prove anything to each other, and we no longer argued about who had changed, and how. We stopped bringing up the past and started having more sex and going on more dates. We started having light conversations that weren't about solving anything.

After two years of intense, heavy conversations, of tiptoeing and of interrogating, now we were just being. Even our children seemed to be thriving. We stopped stifling each other. I went off the antidepressants; they had been helpful, but they were affecting my creativity and output.

Tumi Osei-Tutu was emerging from a personal hell, only to find that

Tumi Morake was soaring to new heights, with or without her at the helm of that name. Who I am when I step into the spotlight is a heightened and slightly less complicated version of myself. A vivacious, naughty character. Tumi Osei-Tutu is more pensive; still fun, but more guarded.

I am glad that I went through all of that for those two years, because what Tumigate and Jacaranda would bring was mere child's play in comparison. I want to be free, and I am free-spirited, but my freedom tastes sweeter with the love of my life by my side.

7

They paid cows;
give them children

After Mpho paid *magadi* (dowry) for me, my mother sat me down and told me to make sure I give him as many babies as he wanted. When I fell pregnant with Bonsu, a couple of months after Mpho and I had our traditional wedding, my mother was overjoyed. But she immediately told me it would have to be a Caesarean birth. I was perplexed. With *my* child-bearing hips? This was not possible! She looked at my feet and said, 'Those size fours are not going to push a big head out. Have you seen the size of Mpho's head?' I just laughed.

In my first trimester, Mpho had to travel to Ghana for a wedding. I stayed behind with my mother-in-law. A few days after Mpho left, I woke up feeling very uncomfortable and realised I was bleeding. In a mild panic I called my mother, who told me to get to a hospital.

My mother-in-law and I went to Johannesburg General Hospital. Yup, before I was 'balling', I was stuck with government hospitals like the average South African. Great doctors, sure – I was at university with a lot of them – but a really shitty process to get to them, past the moody, over-worked, couldn't-give-a-rat's-ass nurses.

My favourite question I was asked that morning was, 'Why are you walking around if you are bleeding?' I actually laughed out loud. When I *eventually* got to a doctor, he had the worst bedside manner I have ever experienced. He clearly wasn't a Wits graduate. Enjoying a fat gossip with one of the nurses, he then examined and injected me without explaining anything. Although he did mention something about an opening to the nurse before turning to leave. I asked him if my baby was okay. He said he had given me something to stop the cervix from opening and that another doctor would come to check on the baby. *Thanks for nothing, asshole,* I thought.

He walked out, and some other shitty nurse walked in and asked if I was done. I said yes, and she told me to go back to the waiting room to wait for the scan. On my way there I began to feel faint, and as the lights went out a male nurse caught me and put me on a bed. He could not understand why I had been allowed to leave the room after being medicated.

I bit my tongue. He was being kind, I was hormonal and the other nurses were working on my last nerve. My mother-in-law, God bless her soul, calmed me down and told me not to take people's bad behaviour personally.

A couple of nurses began looking over at us, and clearly they were discussing me. The heat rose on my face; could they have been more obvious? One of them came over and asked if I had been on TV. I said I had. She turned out to be a fan of our sitcom *Izoso Connexion*, and the 360-degree turnaround in the treatment I then received from them was ridiculous. This confirmed that they were shitty by choice, not by design, and it offended me even more. I never cracked a smile for them, not for a second.

Thank God this was before the advent of camera phones; can you imagine how many unsmiling selfies I would have ended up in? The next doctor – a fellow Witsie – was much kinder and very informative. He explained that my cervix had begun to open but that there was nothing to worry about if I took the medication and stayed off my feet for a bit. Everything looked great as far as he was concerned. I was relieved; the idea of spending any more time than necessary in this place was too daunting.

When Mpho returned from his trip to Ghana, he arrived with a list of names for our son. I was livid. I had wanted to name my first child, and being told that he had pre-existing names that were non-negotiable took the wind out of my sails. I had been obsessing over names, preparing myself for that moment when the heavens would open and an angelic harmony would accompany my heir's name.

Then this guy comes back and gives me a whole history lesson and reveals a trail of names. I was resentful, but I had a few months to get over it. As I was about to become an Osei-Tutu, I would respect the wishes of my new family. Then Mama called me one morning to tell me my son's name – Onalenna. She sounded quite amped about it.

Kwaku Mensah Bonsu Onalenna was born in March 2009, via C-section. I was so glad that my mother and I didn't take bets on this one, because I had been convinced I would push this kid out. But there I was, huge as a house when we packed our bags and headed to the hospital. I started freaking out. Exactly *where* the baby would be coming *from* had never been at the front of my mind, but now I began to imagine my poor coochie being stretched to accommodate that enormous head. All those childbirth videos played in my mind. I decided, there and then, that I would definitely be asking for drugs.

We headed to Netcare Rand Clinic in Hillbrow. Private, but cheap. We did not have medical aid, and the only government hospital I was willing to give birth in was in Thaba Nchu. I never went into full-on labour. I just went through what felt like period pains and that was that. My boy was chilling in there, enjoying womb service, so we had to evict him by force.

My son, the chief, was ushered into the world by the best in the business, or so I'm told. I had three experienced doctors, all around my father-in-law's age, who apparently only made rare appearances. The sister who was in charge of my ward even asked who I was to have these guys tending to me. The anaesthetist was a Ghanaian (an old acquaintance of my father-in-law's), as was the obstetrician, and only the paediatrician was South African.

I went through what felt like death as they cut me and went in for the baby, and when I heard him cry, I inhaled as if I had not breathed for a long time. I felt beautiful, cool air filling my lungs, and my heart was bursting. I was a mother. To an alien. Come on, you can't tell me you look at newly born babies and think 'beautiful'. They don't even look human. But this was the most beautiful alien I had ever seen. He was really tiny at 2.4 kilograms, but I breastfed the heck out of him, and by the time we left the hospital he had put on 200 grams. Yup, I was a good cow.

I had a major gig coming up in July, and I needed to get myself performance fit. However, I was expected to wait for three whole months before I could leave the house, and the baby was not allowed out for another three. It really makes no sense when you consider that the baby regularly leaves the house within that period for check-ups, but for all my rebelliousness, I am obedient when it comes to the wishes of my elders and anything they deem customary. Their wish was for me to be at my grandmother's place for those first three months, and so I obliged – within reason.

As I had just had major surgery, Mama and I waited six weeks before travelling to Thaba Nchu. She had come to Johannesburg to support me through the birth. Her driver's licence had expired years before, so I drove. I was breastfeeding on demand, so I didn't get much sleep, and this drive, for all intents and purposes, was a bad idea. Halfway to Thaba Nchu I experienced what I can only describe as a temporary blackout.

My mother and baby were asleep in the back. Their sleep must have been contagious, because I went off the road. A bakkie behind me saw everything and stopped to check that we were all right. Oom Johan was very concerned. He suggested that I take some time and head back to Ventersdorp before driving out again. But I decided to continue the journey. My adrenalin was pumping and I decided to ride it out. My mother had bruised her head on the baby seat but Bonsu was fine, just screaming from being bounced around. I was shaken too, but nobody was badly hurt and I needed to get to Thaba Nchu. For the first time, I felt that perhaps we were forcing matters, but I had made the commitment and was already halfway there.

It was probably one of my most meaningful trips. When we eventually got to the gate, my uncle came out and rubbed sand from the yard on Bonsu's forehead as a sign that he was on home ground and to let the ancestors know that he had arrived. My grandmother was in her bed waiting for him. We sat there, with her cradling my son, and my mother sitting at the foot of the bed, four generations in one room. A rare thing. A beautiful thing.

I had an intense but spiritually fulfilling month of *mabele* breakfasts and tea in bed. I requested samp from my uncle, who makes the best in the family; none of his sisters come close. He made me the heartiest one. I would leave there fatter than ever and so happy. However, I missed my husband, and I missed being out in the world.

In no time at all, I was negotiating an early release. My mother-in-law also missed us, which made the appeal to my family that much easier; after all, I was her daughter now, an Osei-Tutu, and my family had to comply with her wishes. I still had a month before the Cape Town trip, and I was relieved to get some real prep and rest time at home.

So I went back to Joburg and started looking at my notes to figure out a hot fifteen minutes for my first Vodacom Comedy Festival. Four weeks of comedy, and more money than I had ever made in my comedy career. After maternity leave, it was a welcome relief. Bonsu was small and I was still breastfeeding, but luckily I had married the best man for my kind of job. Mpho wasn't about to let me pass up this career opportunity, so he joined us in Cape Town. He spent his time attending local castings and doing freelance radio and TV voice-over work. He was also working primarily as a writer, a job you can do anywhere.

My admiration and respect for him grew immensely. He was so committed to his roles as a father and partner that he was willing to make the move solely to help me with our baby. Thanks to him, I got to do the Vodacom Festival, my reputation grew in comedy circles, and I began the intricate dance between motherhood and career.

Lesedi was born in 2012, three years after Bonsu. This pregnancy came as a nice surprise. I had gone in for blood tests for insurance purposes, and was told I was pregnant. It was great news in a dark time in my life: I had just buried my mother two months before, and I was still in shock.

This was a busy and sometimes punishing pregnancy. I was emotionally exhausted and happy to keep busy so as not to dwell on the great loss I had suffered. However, I also wanted to be in the best shape for the baby, which presented me with multiple challenges. For one, I was in my first trimester and on a roadshow travelling between nine provinces in three weeks. It was one of those gigs that had been booked months in advance, so there was no getting out of it.

I also experienced severe morning sickness. The only food I could keep down was Ghanaian cuisine, mainly fried fish, *shito* (a sauce made from smoked fish, chilli and palm nut oil) and *kenkey* (a West African sourdough that is basically fermented maize wrapped in corn leaves). Everything else I had to eat with caution. I puked on planes and lived on ginger biscuits.

I seemed to be surrounded by the one thing that made me sick as hell – coffee. Honestly, this pregnancy really highlighted how much coffee people consume, especially in the corporate world I was working in.

Luckily I had the most generous client, who upgraded me at every hotel and insisted I join his team in the airport lounges. He had just lost his son in a motorcycle accident, and I had just lost my mother, so we clicked. He was a thoughtful man, the kind I like to call 'user-friendly'. Although he was really holding himself together, his loss had clearly broken him. I would notice him doing his best to hold on, but losing his grip in quiet moments.

The man moved me, as I could not imagine the loss of a child. I had a child and another on the way, and the thought that you cannot protect them from harm scared me. Connecting with other people's pain is powerful. It somehow eases yours, making your experience feel less lonely.

In this situation, the moments of good laughter were made so much sweeter, like catching deep breaths in between suffocating pain. When showtime came, we made our presentations with finesse despite what we were going through. We did what needed to be done.

I was still doing gigs by the time I was as big as a house and ready to pop. It helped me cope with the pain of losing my mother. I was on top of my comedy game and addicted to the stage. I loved it; it made me feel more alive than ever. This time I got myself a doula so we could try for a VBAC – vaginal birth after Caesarean. I was told any healthy pregnancy had a good chance of ending in a VBAC, so I figured, why not?

Rosalia was amazing. She prepared me mentally and spiritually and, with Sue, midwife extraordinaire, they were ready to help me realise my dream. I had never experienced a natural birth, and this was my second chance at it. Women who have been through the torment might think I must have been off my head to want it, but I did. I wanted to feel what it was like to have nature tell you, 'It is time.'

I went into labour at Eastgate Mall just as Mpho and I we were about to catch a movie. I thought I was experiencing Braxton Hicks contractions – false labour. But the contractions became more regular and more painful, and when I didn't even have the strength to spit out expletives, I knew I was really in labour. Mpho rushed me home and we called Rosalia. She made me run a bath to see if things might ease up.

But they only got worse. The hospital where I wanted to give birth was full, so we had to go to the alternative, Linkwood. When we got there, I was sure I was five to death. I wanted to hold onto something and touch nothing at the same time. I wanted to vomit and pull this thing out of me. Mpho held my hand through it all and told me to breathe. I would have kicked him if my whole body wasn't preoccupied with comrade womb's pain. I felt as if my brain was flipping all the switches in my body to find the off button for the contractions, but failing miserably.

Then a weird thing began to happen – the contraction times kept changing. My doula already suspected that there could be a problem and had called the gynae. When she'd checked how dilated I was, she could hardly fit two fingers in there, even though the contractions were in full swing. The baby's heart rate was getting slower, and she chose not to take any chances.

She told the gynae that I needed a Caesarean. Then she high-fived me and called me a champ for trying for a natural birth, but said that the baby was in distress and we had to get it out. You think comrade womb got the memo? Nope. The contractions continued, and now that I knew we weren't pushing, I demanded drugs.

So I experienced a natural labour, and let me tell you, I will not be making any requests for it again. Although I was disappointed that I could not give birth naturally, I was grateful that it wasn't my fault that I was not bringing my child into the world the way my mother had delivered me. It clearly wasn't meant to be.

Mpho stayed by my side throughout and tried to remain cheerful while the theatre was being prepped and we waited for the paediatrician to arrive. It was a laugh a minute, even through the pain. I was asking all kinds of questions: Couldn't I just get a hit of morphine or marijuana, seeing as this was a medical emergency?

Mpho complained that his hand was hurting from my grip; I asked him if it felt like labour. Eventually we made it into the theatre, and I have never offered up my back so willingly to a giant needle. I needed this pain to stop. It felt life-threatening. They promised me that it wasn't, but I didn't believe them for shit.

As the drugs started kicking in and that familiar warmth crept over the lower half of my body, I began to relax, but my blood pressure kept rising instead of dropping. I overheard the nurse tell the anaesthetist, and he said that this was not supposed to be happening. I looked him dead in the eye and asked him if he'd passed his medical exams with 50 per cent or with a distinction, so that I would know whether I should worry or not.

Ah, we had fun. I don't know what other rubbish I spoke, but the sister assisting me said that she had had the best laugh in that delivery room. I promised to send her an invoice, as it had all been at my expense.

I was surrounded by warm, accommodating people who must have known how scared I was, wielding my comedy sword in defence. Humour definitely kept me from panicking. Before I knew it I had been cut open and my baby swiftly lifted from my belly. But there was more bad news: my belly was dark green with meconium, the poop babies release when they are in distress in the womb. My baby had really been in trouble. You know how people who are scared crap themselves? Well, apparently you can shit yourself in the womb, too! The fun conversation stopped, and Rosalia was at my head, talking to me. Mpho cut the umbilical cord, and when my boy finally cried, I cried too. He had made it safely into the world.

Back in the ward, though, he did not take to the breast. Rosalia expressed foremilk from my breasts (sore sore sore) and fed the baby. I was getting frustrated and my baby was not okay. His fontanelle was swollen. The paediatrician took him from me and I fell asleep. When I woke up, the doctor had taken him to the Neonatal Intensive Care Unit (NICU), where he was being fed through a tube in the nose. They suspected an infection.

This scared me. He was tiny, only two kilograms. I was told not to worry, but to pump as much milk as I could. And I didn't worry until I went to see him in the NICU. He had so much wiring attached to him, and I could barely look at those tubes in his nose. I pumped milk every time my breasts felt even remotely full and kept taking milk to the ward. I made sure my little boy never had to take formula.

When I was discharged from the hospital, I found out that they had beds available, so I paid to stay there. I could not bear the idea of going home without my baby. I spent so many hours in the NICU that the nurses kept having to ask me to leave. Nana Yaa visited and would sanitise her hands and stick them into the incubator to massage my baby while gently speaking to him. After a week, I was allowed to enter and wipe him

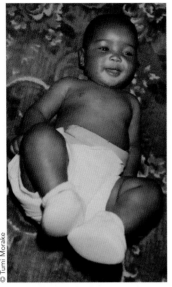

A family picture from happier times: Mama, me and Papa

Me, at six months

That laugh! Mama loved being a nurse

Mama in the seventies. Ah, those legs, which she claimed I also have. They have yet to be seen

© Tumi Morake

© Tumi Morake

Mama's first car. I'm told she was the first woman driver in her 'hood

Sitting with my favourite human at the time, at our home in Mafikeng

© Tumi Morake

© Tumi Morake

Crèche. Mama showed up for every event and special occasion

Me and baby Vonani in 1990

Mmabatho High, class of '99. From left: Paul, Tshepo, me and Dise

With my grandmother at her ninetieth birthday celebration

Babymoon in Egypt. Our last holiday before being married with kids

My grandmother and one-month-old Bonsu

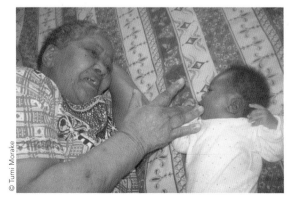

My new in-laws. From left: Mme Mahlape, Mpho, me, Nana Yaa and Ntate Tony in his Royal Kente cloth

© Fani Mahuntsi

© Tumi Morake

My first Vodacom Comedy Festival; the biggest show of my career at the time. I had just breastfed Bonsu, who was backstage being burped by Dad

© Tumi Morake

Graduation day at Wits, 2011. The happiest and saddest day, because Mama could not be there

With Nana Yaa at the 2010 FIFA World Cup

Pregnant with number three and wrapping up season two of *Kota Life Crisis* in late 2013

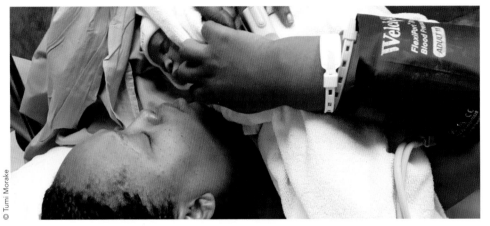

The day I had my last baby, my princess Afia

The 2015 Cape Town Funny Festival in London. From left: Siv Ngesi, Alan Committie, me, Carl Wastie and Marc Lottering

A moment with David Kau after I won the Comics' Choice Comic of the Year Award in 2016

somizi   ...

With 4 472 361 (round it up to 4.5mil) @somizi and @tumi_morake are the highest rated hosts for the @TheSAMAs in the last 10 years. 👍

SOUTH AFRICAN MUSIC AWARDS

#SAMA23 HOSTS

SOMIZI MHLONGO

TUMI MORAKE

Somizi warned me to strengthen my spirit and brace myself for success. Then we did this!

© Tumi Morake

Flexing my theatre muscle with an original play by Vanessa Frost, Jose Domingos and me

© Tumi Morake

Starting in February 2017, I hosted two seasons of *Red Cake* with Alan Committie

© Tumi Morake

A light moment with the late Hugh Masekela on the set of *Bantu Hour*

© Tumi Morake

At home at CliffCentral for the *Sipping Tea* podcast with my on-air partner Mabale Moloi. I should never have left

© Tumi Morake

I miss these moments at Jacaranda FM with Martin Bester

© Tumi Morake

'Anger around Tumi intensifies'. I never got used to seeing headlines like these

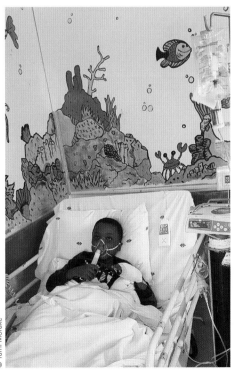

© Tumi Morake

While the fires raged at Jacaranda, I was in this quiet place, supporting my baby Bonsu

The scariest day of my life. I realised how incredibly blessed I am

© Tumi Morake

© Tumi Morake

I was home for the first time in three months when we took this picture

© Kevin Mark Pass

The Three Musketeers. They keep me grounded. Bonsu the sage, Lesedi the jester and Afia the confidant

© Tumi Morake

Accra, Ghana, with my family. From left: Ntate Tony, Lesedi, Mpho, Bonsu, me, Afia and Mme Mahlape

down and change his nappies. He had to undergo a lumbar puncture among other things, but he was slowly recovering. This kid was my hero.

By week two, he had fewer wires and gadgets around him. The nurse encouraged me to try breastfeeding him. I put him on, took a deep breath and held him for a while before I began trying. I expressed a little milk, and ran my nipple under his nose. He parted his lips. I put the nipple to his lips and he sucked it in, quick and hard, and began drinking. My lungs filled with the same cool, soothing air I had felt when I heard Bonsu's first cry, and I began sobbing uncontrollably. I had been so scared, so worried, so eager for my baby, and here he was, drinking like a thirsty giant.

My baby gained the weight he needed to reassure the paediatrician that he was making a full recovery. He had no official names yet, because we did not want to name him before he had left the hospital and we could have the naming ceremony, but he was already 'Kwabena' by virtue of being born on a Tuesday and 'Manu' for being the second boy to arrive.

In church, Mpho had heard the word 'light' in Sesotho and English and decided that it was a sign, so he named our son 'Lesedi'. Vonani and I decided on 'Aobakwe' – 'praise Him'. Nana Yaa visited me some days later and arranged his names in the official papers that would be filed at Home Affairs. We would only call him by his names at the actual naming ceremony, but bureaucracy had to happen too. So, we went home with our little Kwabena, 'Tuesday Boy', after two weeks in NICU. His older brother was ready and waiting to play with him.

During all this, I had stopped checking the calendar. A couple of months before, I had signed a contract to host the untelevised night of the South African Music Awards (SAMAs). When we came out of hospital, the SAMAs were a week away, and I could not pull out; my manager at the time did not give me that option. So, the naming ceremony took place shortly after we got home.

Nana Yaa was the last to arrive for it. I was irritable and did not take it well that she was late, especially since I was not willing to start without her. Thankfully, she came bearing more food for the occasion. She recited Max Ehrmann's 'Desiderata', and we heard our son's names as she had arranged them: Aobakwe Kwabena Manu Lesedi. We hugged. She held Lesedi and played with Bonsu. When she said goodbye to everyone, she told her mother and her peers to keep in touch with each other and to get together more often. She made up with a friend of mine with whom she'd fallen out at my wedding.

That was the last time we saw Nana Yaa alive. She spent a couple of days in Cape Town catching up with a good friend, before making her way to the Karoo for AfrikaBurn. On her way to the Burn, she called us: 'This is the last time I can talk to you this side,' she said. 'Tell my nephews I love them—' and then the phone cut out.

So ended my final conversation with the woman who taught me to celebrate my intelligence, to do something special each birthday because each new year counts, and to stop being afraid of being honest with people. I can still hear her laugh and say, 'Aww, you,' if I said something nice about her. She laughed and smiled easily and was an adorable nerd. I miss her dearly.

Mpho and I left for Sun City days later. Fresh Caesarean scar and all, I hosted the SAMAs with Tats Nkonzo, and it was a memorable night of music and laughter. We were so well rehearsed, our entire night was as slick as can be. I was on top of the world, with a thoroughly impressed client. Someone compared me to a bag of maize meal because of my dress, and I was fat-shamed like crazy, but it didn't matter – I had totally killed that gig.

The following morning I was on a high when I headed down to breakfast with my babies, husband and nanny in tow. I got some congratulatory love from guests from the night before, including *Idols* judge Randall Abrahams. I was like, *I am one of a rare few who've been complimented by that guy*. As we sat at breakfast, Mpho got a call. He asked the caller what was wrong, then shock came over him. Had he not been sitting down, he would have collapsed. I caught his phone before it landed in his breakfast. On the line, a hysterical voice that sounded like my father-in-law kept repeating, 'She is dead, she is gone. We've lost her, she is gone.'

'You are not making sense!' I shouted, as if my voice would slap sense into him. 'Who is gone?' When he said Nana Yaa, a black hole began to open in my stomach. I asked to speak to my mother-in-law, who told me, with an eerie calm, that they did not know what had happened exactly, something about a heart attack. Losing Nana Yaa created a crack in our lives that has never been filled. A dark haze had engulfed the table, and I left the children with the nanny and grabbed Mpho. He looked completely dazed.

Whatever happened next, Mpho would need space and privacy. Everything moved in slow motion, and the details around me went out of focus. We got back to the hotel room, where I held him. He was not crying, but it looked as if a million thoughts were running through his head. I was shaking, so I called room service, ordered a neat whisky, and explained the urgency of the situation. I began to phone family – I needed to be doing something. Mpho just wanted to go back to Johannesburg. I understood. I began packing, which is what our nanny found me doing when she came in with the kids.

On our way out, we bumped into Tats. I told him what had happened and that we would be leaving. He asked whether he could have our room; we were only due to check out the next day, and he knew someone who needed a room. I remember this because it stunned me out of my autopilot shock. I thought, *Well, damn, I guess life doesn't stop just because someone is grieving.* I wondered if he was being insensitive or just as opportunistic as anyone else would have been. A room at the Cascades was gold, after all. I don't even remember if I gave him the keys, but we never checked out. We just took our things and left.

Mpho insisted on driving. He needed to focus on something. I did not experience that drive. Instead, I was haunted by the wail of his cousins when we phoned them to let them know what had happened. I was anxious to be with Mpho's parents, who were driving back from wherever they were on the road between Johannesburg and Nelspruit. I did not know what to tell Bonsu. And I did not know how to be there for a man who had just lost his friend and only sister.

It had been almost a year since I lost my mother, and I was still emotionally exhausted from that loss and Lesedi's time in the NICU. I made a quiet pact with myself to keep it together for my baby.

When my in-laws arrived, it broke my heart to look at them. Nana Yaa had been her father's most trusted business ally and heir. The bond with her mother went beyond that of a mother and daughter; they were friends, sometimes each other's spiritual guide. They reminded me of how I had been with my own mother, and I still cannot fathom what Mme was feeling in that time. Tears were running down her cheeks, but she was not sobbing. She was relating how the news had arrived and all the information she was trying to gather.

None of it made sense. A post-mortem would later reveal that Nana Yaa had passed away due to a pulmonary embolism. My sister-in-law, aged thirty-three, had died of natural causes. Within weeks of finding this out, Mpho went to see a pulmonologist. He, Bonsu and our daughter Afia all have pulmonary issues, although, thankfully, Afia is now completely off the asthma pump. The possibility that this might be genetic has crossed our minds, but we do not dwell on it. We move forward in faith and have been assured that there are no signs that this deadly clot is something we should worry about.

I cried so much when we lost Nana Yaa that I sometimes wonder if I was crying just for her, or for my mother too. My mother-in-law had lost a daughter, I had lost a mother, and somehow God had given us each other. Death had once again come to play in my close proximity. This time, I was less afraid of its touch.

When we had to wash Nana Yaa's body, I was there to support my mother-in-law. She was overcome with grief, and although there were many well-meaning people around her, I knew that she needed space, and she would need someone to fight for that for her. We gathered in the room: Sia, who had grown up with Nana Yaa and was like a sister to her, her aunts, Mme and me. I put on my gloves and helped with the cleansing and the dressing of the body, all the while chatting with Mme to make sure that she was coping. Then I asked everyone to leave the room so that she could be alone with her baby.

Me? I felt like I had just shaken hands with death and recognised it as one of those neighbours we all have to deal with at some point.

I have a gag about our last-born, Afia, which is actually a true story: she beat the morning-after pill. I am so glad she did. Afia was conceived during the run of *Bitches* at the Lyric Theatre in 2013. My walk-on music was hip-hop that video girls twerk to, and I went on to tell women to twerk for their men. When I got home, Mpho wanted to know why I was asking women to do things for their men that I was not doing for him. Well, that turned into a rather kinky evening, and the next morning we decided I should take the morning-after pill. We wanted a third child, but we had major travel plans in the pipeline and intended to wait until number two was at least three.

Well, Miss Thang had her own ideas. In fact, everything about having Afia was crazy. About a month and a bit after I self-medicated, I had a rather highly alcohol-infused weekend with a friend. She found my hang-over suspiciously over the top and implied that it could be more than that. Two days later, I was still sick, and Mpho suggested I pee on a pregnancy test stick. Every stick I've peed on since 2008 came back positive, so I do not know what science I was relying on when I told him it was probably going to come back negative and I just needed a detox. Well. That evening, I discovered I needed supplements, not a detox.

My obgyn decided to do a post-mortem of the last pregnancy and explore why my babies were so small. What gestational issues had I had? We also discussed the possibility that this would be my last pregnancy. It was about two years since my last, so we were not totally in the red, but we had cut the same wound twice. It made things risky. I was beginning to think that the more I got pregnant, the riskier it seemed to get for me.

I travelled to Edinburgh to perform my one-woman show, *Herstory*, for a month. I had also booked a few club gigs for that time and was not about to let the pregnancy slow me down. There would be plenty of getting around, and transport was not cheap. This kick-started my healthy pregnancy. I walked every day, everywhere, and the weather was perfect for walking. I lived at the bottom of town, and my shows were on the top of a hill on the other side of Edinburgh. I shared a flat with Loyiso Gola, the gentlest soul, funny as hell. I watched him perform, and his finesse with that mostly English audience blew me away. I wanted to be as comfortable in my skin as he was.

However, I was performing in the UK for the first time, for a three-week run, and it was a sensory overload on a pregnant, hormonal woman who had to live through every waking moment in pure sobriety. I wept a lot in Edinburgh. I cried when I got a bad review, I cried more when I got a four-star review – one star short of full colours! I cried when I had only seven people in my audience. I cried when I had a full house in my last week. I even cried when Loyiso made me the yummiest peanut-butter fruit shake to keep constipation at bay.

Some comedians from home told me that I was being too honest about Edinburgh in my blogs, and that I needed to upsell the fact that I was having the time of my life, but I did not understand what was so scary about the truth. I had overcome so much in going from unrelatable to four stars and a full house that I was not about to pretend it had all happened easily. It was lots of hard work paying off.

I had the most fun hauling my pregnant ass to comedy clubs and being called back to either headline or get paid after open spots. I put on my big-girl panties and made sure Edinburgh was more than a bucket-list item I ticked off; it had to mean something.

And it did. I took part in conversations with the United Nations and the BBC, and participated in a talk with authors Neil Gaiman and Terry Pratchett. I got to ask Neil Gaiman in person when he would be visiting South Africa to sign some books. I was so star-struck I couldn't think of a more intelligent question – like whether they would attempt another collaboration like *Good Omens*.

I watched *Nirbhaya*, a play about the Indian woman who was gang-raped and assaulted on a bus in India. Stories of abuse from other women were shared, including the chilling account of a burn victim still in search of her son. I was confronted with my own issues of abuse and defilement. I knew I had so much to say, so much to tackle back home. I was surrounded by a variety of activists, including those who were fighting for the release of Pussy Riot in Russia.

I came back to South Africa like an MK soldier, battle-ready from training overseas. I had honed my comedy muscle, but an activist spirit had also been sparked. If I was carrying a girl, I would be bringing a queen into the world. I felt like I *had* to be battle-ready; the world is not kind to women.

We discovered later in the pregnancy that my umbilical cord was not passing food on to my baby, which explained why my babies were so little at birth. We experimented with a blood thinner, and the baby gained weight week on week. The start of my last trimester was pure hell. This baby had practically broken my pelvis; it was as if I had never experienced pregnancy before.

I already knew this would have to be a Caesarean birth, as my scar had been thinning throughout the pregnancy and was dangerously thin half-way through my last trimester. And I could barely walk, or even turn over in bed. I cried each time I had to turn after getting numb from being in the same position for too long. It felt as though a long, ice-cold iron rod was digging into my back through my pelvis. I was on the strongest pain medication a pregnant person can take.

It was supposed to be my healthiest, most active pregnancy, and here I was, bedridden. I ballooned, badly, until I was the heaviest I would ever be – 102 kilograms. I suspected that I was carrying a girl, but we asked the doctor not to tell us the sex of the baby. I badly wanted a daughter, and I was hoping for approval from the Man upstairs. The harrowing experience made me think I was having a girl, as my other two pregnancies had not been this merciless.

Mpho and I had a long, heartfelt conversation about closing the baby factory. He had watched me suffer, and the serious risk I was putting myself through with the scar spooked him. He was happy for us to take semi-permanent precautions. We had the usual discussion: What if you die and my new person wants a child? What if, ten years from now, we want another one?

We agreed that adoption is a thing. I figured, since I would be having surgery to have this baby, we might as well snip and tie there. The doctor agreed. I was not that young, and this was my third. I now regret that decision. Not because I want more children, but because *not* being able to have them breaks my heart. The ability to procreate is such a beautiful, sacred thing, and to have consciously removed it as an option seems too harsh now. My angels mean the world to me, though, and they are surely more than enough.

And so, in 2014, my showstopper arrived: Gagoangwe Afia-Serwaa Pontsho. Gagoangwe was the name of my best friend in high school, and I had admired the name from the first time I heard it; I knew I would one day call my daughter Gagoangwe. Literally, 'not to be touched'. Precious, in other words. My daughter is such a reminder of Nana Yaa, not only in appearance but in her intelligence, her smile and her love for people. She is the one sent here to challenge me, so watch this space.

She is as adorable as she is lethal.

Mpho and I place high importance on how the kids treat each other and the people who come into our home. In many ways, I learn a lot about my own behaviour through them, and I can only become a better person by paying attention. It's why I struggle with the amount of time I have to be away from them.

Bonsu has inherited his father's pulmonary issues, and I have come to know the fear and anxiety of having a child who could stop breathing at any moment. His condition can be controlled, but because I travel so much and I'm busy even when I'm at home, I had to entrust that level of care to the people around me. I had to overcome my guilt about this, because it only made it harder to enjoy my work.

The first time Bonsu was admitted to hospital, I spent the entire day there, except for three hours when I left him with his dad to go to work. I don't know where I got the energy from. I slept on the couch next to his bed and went to another gig the next day. I did not have the kind of management that said, 'Your child needs you, we'll get someone else.' And I did not yet have the spine to stand up for myself. I could have made better choices, but I was still there for my baby.

Bonsu has had two surgeries and been hospitalised twice more. Heck, in the middle of writing this book, I set up office in his room to keep an eye on him after a heavy asthma attack. My house is stocked like a chemist, and it's only Lesedi's name that isn't on any of the bottles. Afia has been admitted to hospital every year for the past three years. Between her and Bonsu, there have been enough steroids and adrenaline to get an athlete banned from competitive sports for life.

When children are sick, they need Mommy and Mommy needs them. I wanted to stop working altogether at one point, when they were tag-teaming on major bouts of asthma attacks. It was a catch-22. If I stopped working, I wouldn't earn enough to pay for the best care possible. They would have me, but not the medical care they needed.

So I split my focus and kept moving. I kept working and became run-down from alternating between work and taking care of them. Without Mpho's support, I would have lost my mind. He was also busy, but we were a team, supported by his parents and our Godsend of a nanny.

My bond with Lesedi is quite different from the one I have with Afia and Bonsu. They were needier children, for health reasons, and probably ended up getting more attention because of that. I have consciously gone out of my way to make Lesedi feel seen, lest he become a hypochondriac in the quest for attention. Lesedi became a source of light for me, from the time I was carrying him.

Even now, he is the most buoyant one in any situation: the party starter, the smiler, the one who is strong as an ox. He never gets sick. It's as if his time in the NICU gave him some kind of super immune system. At the same time, he is so gentle, I sometimes have no idea what to do with him. I don't want to 'man him up' in some twisted attempt to adhere to social constructs and ideas of manhood, but I also don't want him to be a pushover.

It's a fine line, and I am treading it carefully. I hate the idea that my children might need therapy because their mother messed them up. I have to keep reminding myself to repeatedly forgive myself; I act only out of love.

Much like my mother, I will do anything for my children. I cannot imagine life without them. They sustain me in a way I cannot explain, and remind me that I am enough. I am perfectly imperfect, yet God had picked me to bring these special people into the world.

8

I gave you beautiful legs

Whenever people told my mother that I looked like her, she would say, with a smile on her face, 'What? This monkey look like me? Never.' She was quite blunt when she did not approve of one of my 'looks'. When I was dating Mike, I barely wore make-up because he hated make-up, and Mama would say, 'But you look plain. He just doesn't want other guys looking at you. Just apply a little liner and lipstick at least.'

Mama liked a well-put-together woman almost as much as she loved an educated one. When I shaved my head, she said, 'A woman *is* her hair,' forgetting that she herself had rocked a brush cut in her youth. She knew what clothes she looked great in, and she was very particular about her appearance. She couldn't understand how a pretty girl like me (according to her) was not interested in beauty. She also could not understand my obsession with trousers.

She would say, 'I gave you beautiful legs, why do you like to hide them?' My saving grace, she'd say, was that I was a beautiful girl. That made me feel good, and I'd forgive her for trying to make me a girly girl. When I refused to take fashion advice from her, she claimed, 'They used to call me the walking catalogue, remember that.'

Despite all these exchanges, Mama never shamed me. She was just trying to convince me that if I put in a little extra effort, I could be a real head-turner. She knew me well, though, and knew that how I looked was right at the bottom of my list of priorities.

In an interview for the cover of a local magazine, a journalist candidly said, 'You are overweight and aren't the typical pretty girl we see in the industry; what do you attribute your success to?'

I was momentarily gutted. I thought she was, in effect, saying that I did not belong in the industry. All because of my looks. I think it was the matter-of-fact way she said it that stung, as though it was an obvious fact that I was well aware of. But she was right. I probably defy the odds because I do not speak with a private-school or Model C accent, I am not conventionally pretty and I am anything but thin.

In that moment with this journalist, though, I remembered the confidence of the cockroach. A cockroach does not belong in your house or on your table, but there it is, creeping along, in no real rush to get out of your way. Even when it knows its time is nearly up as showers of insecticide envelop it, it stands there, defiant. I guess that is me in the entertainment industry. I have employed the cockroach tactic my whole career, stepping into experimental spaces and trusting that God has me, and that I have this X-factor thing I cannot explain.

Nobody, at any point, has ever made me feel like I fit in. That element of discomfort, like being allowed into the room but not offered a chair, keeps me on my toes. I have never been skinny. And ever since my first-born, I have always been overweight. My weight, though, was never front-of-mind for me. I had a joke or two about my body, but that was textbook self-effacing comedy before I went on the attack and took everyone else out – you know, lull them into thinking you're the target, then turn the gun on them. Even then it was more about celebrating how comfortable I was in my own skin rather than it being an apology for how I looked. I celebrate that I look like African prosperity, not Third World poverty.

When it came to race relations, black people accused me of being too friendly with the whites. My aunt even teased me once and said I was a 'witbroodjie' (slice of white bread), like my grandmother, who was always treated well by white people in the Free State when she was still a domestic worker. She was a cute, well-mannered woman who spoke fluent Afrikaans.

My mom, too, had been called *witbroodjie*, for being a perceived favourite at home. How ironic, then, that whites would find me too 'Black Consciousness'. I did not fit in with anyone, so I carved myself a little niche where people who liked something different could enjoy me. I have never been overly aware of those who don't like me, because they are not my focus. The buttered side of the bread is where the love lives.

I committed to a weight-loss programme in 2016 after my Discovery Vitality test results indicated that I was more than ten years older in health than my actual age. I was shocked. I found it unacceptable that I was rushing to my grave because I wasn't taking care of my health. The signs that it was time for a change were there too. I once collapsed in the middle of a rehearsal. I was on high stilts, and someone caught me halfway to the floor. (Yes, on stilts. I have so many tricks up my sleeve, man; it's part of my industry longevity.)

The doctor said I had the symptoms of someone on the verge of heart failure. Something shifted in me. I was already in therapy, which helped, and this was the extra impetus I needed to kick me into action. I needed to stay alive for my babies. Plus, my life insurance would have sucked for Mpho; it really wasn't going to get him to St. Tropez. I was overworked, undernourished and not prioritising my health. I changed my eating habits. I stuck to a regime and started melting away.

When I got through phase one of my weight loss, the press were all over it. I did not understand the big deal. Had people really been that fixated on my weight?

What I missed about being overweight was reading about my *work* in newspapers rather than frivolous articles on how to lose weight, why I'd lost weight or how lovely I looked. Previously, they had written about how Mpho and I were making it work as a couple in the industry, or getting to know the woman behind the work. But I soon began to buy into the weight-loss hype, and thought that perhaps I was finally being accepted as South African performance royalty.

I could stop abusing Craig Jacobs and Brenda Khambule, who had been making me red-carpet ready and worthy for so long. They are the fashion brother and sister the universe sent me, and they were kind to my pocket as well, but I reckoned that the days of not having other designers look my way would end. Maybe now that I looked like a celebrity, I would start being dressed like one.

Thank goodness that feeling lasted all of one moment. The attention eventually became intrusive. My physical body was overshadowing my body of work. What a waste of nearly a decade of crafting and building a name! So I stopped focusing on my body and got back to crafting. I have since gained some of that weight back (although nothing like before). I realised that a lot of what I do is very personal, from the decision to take on projects that are a gamble, to going on this weight-loss regime. I cannot judge people for what they want to get out of this industry, but I know I am too intelligent and talented to chase trends and social pages. That is not what makes me money or brings me fulfilment.

However, the entertainment industry thrives on building and breaking. I have met and spoken to so many young women who say they look up to me for remaining true to myself no matter how big I get. It feels like I do them an injustice if the message I then send is that you must inevitably bend to the will of those who do not even have your best interests at heart, and try to look like them.

When I was called to audition for *Our Perfect Wedding*, I thought that the production company was genuinely keen for me to present the show, as opposed to the usual practice of putting some auditions on camera to prove that they'd considered all their options before hiring their precast choice. I had been to enough of those.

I asked who else they were seeing, and they were quite forthcoming. I knew then that I would get the gig; the people they mentioned were It girls who did not have the kind of interpersonal skills a show like this needed. Don't judge my comment; I had been to enough events as the one nobody notices and I observed these women. Relating to people was not their thing.

As expected, I landed the gig and thought, *Wow Mama, I made it.* I had always wanted to try my hand at TV presenting, because presenters, essentially, are glorified narrators. Narrators have always been my favourite characters to watch on stage. They take you on a journey, and dictate its course. While the characters *in* the story bring it to life, the narrator adds the spice and guides the story. It is such a powerful position, the omnipresent figure who remains with you from start to finish.

Everything about this show felt right. It was run by women, in a production company owned by a woman many of us had idolised since we were little girls – Basetsana Kumalo. I was already financially comfortable thanks to all the corporate work I was doing, but this would be a creative outlet that might later translate into bums on seats when I performed my one-man shows. I had already become a fan of *My Perfect Wedding* when my predecessor, Phumeza Mdabe, presented it. I found her adorable; I could watch her forever. She would say out loud the things she looked like she was thinking while she kept it polite and at arm's-length with her subjects.

While this was happening, Mpho and I were going full-steam ahead with the production of *Kota Life Crisis*. I was producing on weekdays and shooting the wedding show on weekends. It looked like I was winning at life. What I went through on *OPW*, however, would prove to be worse than any treatment I had ever received at the hands of my male counterparts in the industry.

My last-born had just turned a year old and I was quite heavy. I was comfortable in my own skin, but I wanted to lose weight because I was now quite unhealthy. The weight loss was about health, not looks. For some reason I have always believed myself to be quite attractive. Sexy, in fact. And as a comedian, writer and MC, I had never been told that my weight was an issue. It only ever cropped up on social media or at family gatherings, but never quite as humiliatingly as it did when I presented this show.

I already knew that Black Twitter mercilessly ripped off that show. I thought that would be my only battlefield; I did not know I had a whole battle ahead of me in the production house itself. Preposterous comments flew back and forth between the execs and production about my body and the intense work that needed to go into hiding my big belly. This despite the fact that the show had been on air for a few weeks and I could already tell that the audience was warming to me. Audiences are creatures of habit. They are resistant to change, but if you deliver, they come round. This was the case with me; I was getting increasingly comfortable and making the show my own.

However, the feedback I got from the people who had hired me made me wonder if I was missing something. They were not exactly blown away by my work; my body was distracting them. It was like they just suddenly realised how overweight I was. But I did not get fat on the show; I had arrived fat. Did they not know what I looked like before they hired me? I chose to focus on fine-tuning my presenting skills. Most of the audience was already enjoying my cheeky sense of humour and my relatability. Of course there were those who disliked change, and a few just generally disliked me, which happens. That's just how life is. But I was not noticing enough fat-shaming online to make me think that my body was a crisis for the production company.

Eventually, my stylist was changed. I was not surprised. I think the poor soul was overwhelmed, and the clothes she put me in had mostly been disappointing. They smacked of a poor budget and were quite … ordinary, certainly not up to the standard I had come to appreciate watching the previous season of the show. I therefore assumed that the stylist's choice of clothing was the problem, until I was told that the designers from the previous season were hesitant to dress me because I was overweight. Fair enough. Their business.

However, I now avoid those labels like the plague, even after my weight loss. If I wasn't good enough then, consider me still not good enough now. One of the women from the production company (I was floored when she turned out to be as hefty as I was) had to be there in person to oversee this wardrobe process. Small budget, big-budget demands.

A new stylist, Mimi (Millicent Nkangane), the magician behind Mimi Spunk, was brought to our downtown studios for a fitting. Mimi had dressed all shapes and sizes and came highly recommended by the producer. She was the silver lining in this whole process and wasn't there to fix ugliness, but to figure out what looked great on me and what I liked. As for me, I wanted clothes that would help me do my job better and look good on screen.

I loved Mimi's clothes and the way she saw me, as well as her ideas for where we could go with my new look. The producer, executive producer and commissioning editor arrived to observe the fitting, so I made one of the dressing rooms available so that we could all be accommodated comfortably. In this room I was spoken to, and about, as if I wasn't present. I got a real taste of body-shaming, but I took it on the chin. I heard things like 'But we need to cover that stomach', and 'Her stomach is a problem.' I knew I was quite heavy after having my baby, but this felt unnecessary.

The make-up lady had brought wigs for me to try on, and I remember the executive producer saying 'no' in the most affronted tone. I felt like an ugly duckling that needed a major makeover. I laughed when they said, 'No, we can't have Twitter attack her for that.' I could take the Twitter insults, but the things they were saying in the room cut me more. Even my natural hair came under fire.

I realised that I had inherited the show from a beautiful, thin host who could wear anything, but that did not warrant their attempt to 'fix' how I looked. There weren't that many people insulting my looks on Twitter to warrant being subjected to this level of humiliation. I took it, though – anything to make the show look good.

Personally, I thought they had cut corners in the beginning by employing the cheapest stylist they could get, and they got what cheap will get you. All they had to do was appoint a stylist who knew what she was doing and we would all win. I was not the problem. I had been in magazines, on stage and on TV before. I knew I was not the problem. I just wish I had repeated that to myself in the moment. Thick-skin loading.

One of the cast members was next door, overhearing the entire exchange. When everyone had left, she came in and hugged me. She was shocked at how I had been spoken to and could not believe how gracious I had been. I felt like a toddler who'd fallen down. As a parent, if you say nothing and just look away, the toddler tends to just get up, decide it wasn't so bad and gets on with life. But if you react and rush to fix the booboo, they realise it hurts, and they start wailing. My cast member had pointed at my booboo, and it hurt. I swallowed the tears. Although I did not deserve to be treated that way, I wanted them to be done with it so I could go back to producing my eight-times-nominated sitcom. I made it my goal to be the best damn host that show had ever had, so that by the time I left, the women who'd insulted me would remember my talent and not the fat that they decided mattered above all else.

I left the show after two seasons, and there was an overwhelming demand for my return. I felt like I had won. My worth had been taken into account and nothing they threw at me could break me.

For the most part, though, I had a great time on *OPW*. I met beautiful souls, made new friends and learnt a lot about human nature. I cried behind closed doors with a lot of brides, about stuff I could never share on air.

One bride was coming out of an abusive relationship and marrying the guy who had supported her through it. Some were marrying questionable guys but needed the wedding to save face. There were couples who were so in love that everything around them disappeared when they looked at each other. Some even planned to secretly rendezvous on the eve of their wedding. I chatted to fathers who were not ready to let their daughters go. Although they refused to share their vulnerability on camera, I was honoured that they trusted me enough to share their feelings with me.

Of all the grooms, only two acted dodgy right in front of my eyes. One outright flirted with me, and the other had a final fling the night before his wedding. We also had to dump a wedding in the middle of a shoot because the priest condemned the filming of the wedding and threatened not to marry the couple.

There was so much drama on *OPW* that it deserved its own behind-the-scenes show. I got to see, first-hand, a woman completely devastated by her husband, a compulsive liar. My heart broke for her. I watched as her one dream, a dream that every little girl has, was yanked out of her hands. It was a tragedy to behold. We stayed with her long after the cameras stopped rolling. There were situations where we just couldn't do the job any more. We are human, after all, and we had to be sensitive to the circumstances.

We didn't just follow the drama of the wedding; we cared about the people involved. I grew up on that show, and in some ways I also found myself. I realised I wanted to make the kind of TV that connected me to people on a personal level. We weren't changing lives or anything like that, but love was presented in different packages. Great weddings versus great marriages were playing out, and I got to be the observer, playfully taking the audience through the events. I would incorporate quotes, proverbs or lines of poetry into my opening monologue, based on the pre-interview information I was given.

I learnt that love was as simple as it was complicated. I met a couple where the man loved the bottle, and acted aloof when left to his own devices. His bride-to-be was more focused and ambitious. When he was with her, he genuinely seemed to have purpose, and when he wasn't, he was like an idling car waiting to be driven. It was interesting to observe. Anyone would have thought that she was wasting her time and he was being controlled. Instead, they were textbook yin and yang. They complemented each other perfectly. Another lesson in love came in the form of a taxi driver who was marrying the love of his life. The catch was that she had been underage when they started dating. This caused an uproar on social media and even hit the newspapers.

The man in question was mobbed outside his home following the broadcast. There were calls for him to be arrested for statutory rape. I was upset when this happened, because I had warned my director about the issue and asked that he consult with the producer. I asked that we not mention the fact that she was fifteen when they hooked up because, by both their admissions, she had lied to him about her age. At the time of their wedding, she was in her mid-twenties and they were still going strong. I felt that, in a country where we cannot romanticise older men preying on younger women, this love story should never have included that detail.

That said, these things are complicated. There are so many 'controversial' couples who have stood the test of time despite their age differences. The two people in question clearly loved each other and had started a family long after their dodgy hook-up, so I felt that the groom was taking the blame for all the creeps out there and not just for his own sins. The couple's wedding was marred by the negative press, which could have been avoided, and my heart broke for them.

The logistics of the show humbled me. I had to pack my ego away in my luggage, as I often had to change in the production vehicle or on the road, at crazy hours while coaxing tight-lipped families into talking to us. Trying to find decent ablutions was like playing *Where's Wally?* on some of the rural shoots, and the hours were gruelling. You know what? I enjoyed every second of it. I had a great rapport with the crew and learnt that I am a natural team player. I believe it translated into what people saw and enjoyed on TV.

Ironically, the show nearly cost me my marriage. I was seeing less and less of my family, and I would share my experiences with my colleagues but not with my husband. When I brought up the issue of body-shaming,

Mpho did not understand why I allowed it to get to me when I had been so comfortable with my body before.

Then he said, 'If you don't like your body, do something about it.'

He was right. The downside, though, was that he said this at a time when I needed to hear something else. Something comforting. He was so used to me being thick-skinned that I don't think he saw how much it hurt to be reduced to my appearance.

Perhaps it was because I had not been giving him any attention. I missed my children and being at home, so when I was there I would focus on them, and not Mpho. I was so distracted, so torn, needing to keep up with my children and completely neglecting the man who had gifted me those babies in the first place. The timing of my permanent exit from *OPW* could not have been better.

9

Ha wa mpha sheleng

(*You did not give me ten cents*)

Every time I got upset with Mama for repeating something I'd told her in confidence, or she'd say something that I felt was inappropriate, she would reply, '*Ha wa mpha sheleng*' (You did not give me ten cents), meaning I had not paid her to keep quiet. Once, when she revealed a family secret during one of her manic-depressive episodes, I asked what had got into her, and that was her response.

A lot of people called Mama mad for the things she said – she spoke many a truth in jest, or she'd touch on thorny subjects in her loud, deep voice, and people's response would be, '*Ausi Tebogo ke setseno waitsi*' (sis Tebogo is crazy). Often, one would be confused about *how* she had got onto the topic. Her conversations detoured a lot; I seem to have inherited that disjointed thought pattern. Half the time when I start off, I go off on a tangent and completely forget where I was meant to be going with the thought. You can only imagine what a challenge writing this book has been.

My mother's funeral was a reminder of what the country's fight for freedom had cost her, my father and our family, and it is also the reason why I am as outspoken as I am. I used to let people have their say and only occasionally spoke up. Usually, I had to be pushed to open my mouth. After she died, I realised she had spoken without fear or favour, and that it was a good thing.

When people speak about apartheid, they tend to do so in general terms rather than in a focused discussion. Apartheid is like a blanket, a filthy blanket that covers up the ecosystem crawling beneath it. I find it sad that the different races can be so glib about it – black people who have grown tired of the topic, and white people who won't even talk about it anymore because 'it's been over twenty years now; get over it'.

I can't get over it. In fact, if I ever got over it, it would be like spitting in the faces of those who had fought so long for our liberation. I spent more than six years working with schools around the country, and I saw what effects the apartheid education had on generations of students. There's the black handyman at my flat in Yeoville who would go down on his knees every time he went to see the white superintendent in his flat, and that man never asked the black man to get off his knees. It is painful to observe black people who feel inferior to white people, and white people who assume they may speak on behalf of black people.

Some view apartheid as an event that came and went. They refuse to acknowledge that it was a system deliberately developed by a small minority so that they could thrive at the expense of the majority. We choose to ignore how we lived in a country where a minority was served by a suppressed majority.

A friend of mine told me about an old man who tried to explain the lingering effect apartheid has on some people's mentality. He said it is like a goat that is tied to a pole with a short rope. The goat will walk around the pole on the short rope and get used to the limited movement and space. Then, when you untie it, it will continue to walk in that limited space, as if it is still tethered to the short rope. That is the trap that apartheid was; there are people who are still walking in that small circle, unaware of anything better. So, what the actual fuck do you mean when you say 'get over it'?

I won't try to write an academic analysis of apartheid; I lived it. I watched the Nelson Mandela biopic *Long Walk to Freedom*, and I wept when I watched Zindzi visiting her father in prison for the first time. I had lived that. I understood what it felt like – I was separated from my parents because of the system. Today we have schools where teachers who learnt the wrong things from teachers who were taught the wrong things continue teaching the wrong things to students. We are quick to criticise the government for the sad state of education and forget that we started in the negative integers and are now trying to catch up with the beneficiaries of the system. For every ten rand spent on white education in the past, black people had to share a fraction of that with coloured people and Indians. But no, get over apartheid.

There are families who, to this day, are trying to find each other because they were torn apart by the system. Relatives killed, gone into hiding. My father worked and fought with many comrades with incredible stories to tell, which I got to hear first-hand. The Truth and Reconciliation Commission was great PR, but it did very little for us. There were people who got away with so much; there were families who walked away with more questions than answers.

There was no closure, only frustration. I wish we had focused more on how we would move forward together than on how we were going to forgive and forget. The fact that a white man can still publicly say that apartheid was not a crime against humanity shows you how the TRC had failed us. It is as if we had all suddenly woken up to find that the struggle was over and it was every man for himself in this new South Africa, because we'd supposedly all kissed and made up.

Now is the time to build, we were told. On what foundation? We can't get over apartheid just because it has been abolished and some of us are living cushy lives.

The biggest issue, if you want to understand my seeming obsession with apartheid, is that its hateful mentality continues to this day. One has only to visit Cape Town as a person of colour to experience the lingering fart of apartheid. I was in Franschhoek with my husband, watching the coloured receptionist recalibrate her racism when I started speaking and she realised that we weren't tourists. It was like a double-take of sorts – she had welcomed us warmly, but now her tone changed as she awkwardly handed us over to her black male colleague without even saying, 'So and so will take care of you.'

The colleague laughed when I remarked that the receptionist probably assumed we were foreigners. I was amused rather than mad. I should have let Mpho speak first. As we've often been told, 'he speaks so well'. In fact, I often ask Mpho to make the phone bookings so that his 'Anglo-Blaxon' accent can get us in. Nana Yaa started using 'Angela' instead of her first name because, combined with her accent, it made for a winning combination and got her through the door.

But no, let's get over apartheid. I had to listen to a white Afrikaans guy explain to me why quotas were hurting rugby. He complained that Afrikaners have a rich rugby history and have groomed their kids to play for the Boks, only for them to be rejected because they are not black. I have to stomach women with half my intellect talking down to me ... until they see me interact with their CEOs and realise that they punch above their weight in taking me on.

What do you mean when you say 'get over it'? Let's not even go deep; what does it mean on an everyday level? What does 'get over it' mean when a white woman can walk into a shop and interrupt the assistant serving me, without apology, and expect the man to drop everything and help her? What does 'get over it' mean when I get scolded for not assisting a customer in a shop I don't work in? I wasn't even dressed like CNA staff when this Caucasian lady said that maybe I should stop looking at the books and actually help customers. Why?

Because black people don't read, so I couldn't possibly have been reading? Why is there a look of surprise on some people's faces when they are told that I read extensively? We are struggling to bring down the superiority complex of a minority and the inferiority complex of a majority.

Every time I argue with my paternal aunt about her insistence on voting for the ANC, she says, 'I am scared that if I don't, apartheid will come back.' On the other side of the fence is the white narrative, which proves that the heartbeat of apartheid is still alive and well. Do yourself a favour and Google 'squatter camps in South Africa'. The results create the impression that the majority of people living in squatter camps are white.

I resent the implication that white people have been pushed to the sidelines – it is this kind of claim that feeds into the 'white genocide' narrative. I can't stomach it. Their attempt at claiming that they are the victims of reverse apartheid is ridiculous. Also, let's be fair: our government hardly has the ability or expertise to get that right. It took us ages to oust a corrupt president, and we've barely weeded out his cohorts, yet you think the government can eradicate an entire race? Come on.

The people who attacked me from the second I arrived at Jacaranda will read the preceding paragraphs as me saying I hate Afrikaners and/or white people. No. Read again. Get a translator if you must, because I am convinced so much got lost in translation. *It's apartheid I fucking hate.* I hate it because it has become a gag all these years after it was abolished. I hate it because it seems, according to someone who ran to the Broadcasting Complaints Commission of South Africa (BCCSA) and claimed that I was too young during apartheid to be affected by it, that only an elite few are allowed to speak about it.

Must be nice, hey, to have your privilege run so deep that, as someone who benefited from apartheid, you now get to allocate speaking roles too. I hate it, because there are people walking around with a superiority complex that they refuse to challenge. Even by themselves, alone in their corners, they won't look inward and question where their thinking comes from.

Our country has been pussyfooting around this issue for so long that it makes for yummy content in comedy. Comedy thrives on society's bugbears, taboos, things we are all thinking about but are too afraid to say out loud. Or it offers you an opportunity to expose the ridiculousness of the things we fear the most. Apartheid. Racial hatred and tension.

That kind of shit that makes no sense, because we all breathe the same damn air, love the same things more often than not, and are pretty much stuck here together because we know there's no better place to be. I do not care how much you may object: South Africa is that girl you know you will always love and should have married. Even if you end up with someone else, you keep longing for her. That is my South Africa.

I had hoped that jumping onto the Jacaranda FM platform would be an opportunity to laugh and reflect on this South Africa, which I share with so many people. A lot of us get pushed into corporate spaces, work spaces, schools and other spaces that throw us into each other's faces across race and culture. I thought a radio station with a listenership as diverse and seemingly proudly South African as Jacaranda would be ripe for some self-effacing comedy. I clearly misjudged the target so badly, I hit an innocent bystander chomping merrily on his *koeksister*.

Tumigate was the first time I saw the ugly side of post-apartheid South Africa. In HD. My material on *Breakfast with Martin Bester and Tumi Morake* had already rubbed people up the wrong way. The conversation that happened on 12 September 2017 was just the final straw they had been waiting for. And, boy, did they lap it up. The frustrated and voiceless suddenly felt heard, and had an outlet. It was as if they had taken a laxative and I held the key to the toilet. When they let rip, it was a stinker.

So, what happened that fateful day? Did I snap? Was I *looking* for a fight with white people? Or did I just get ahead of myself? Nah, it was a regular day at the office with the usual racist bile slipping onto the breakfast page's timeline with nobody batting an eyelid. I was getting used to it. It was like a dripping tap at night, making a faint sound that can become background noise, even ambience. But in the dead quiet, that dripping will start irritating the shit out of you; you will fling off your blanket and figure out a way to stop that damn dripping or try to muffle the sound.

The drip was loud that day, and there was a tense atmosphere between the different team members. We were a clash of personalities peppered with racial tension. My colleagues were not overtly racist, but we were a diverse lot from different social and racial backgrounds. At Jacaranda, we were sharing a space where voice and narrative are part and parcel of the workplace, so the minute anyone felt silenced or controlled, a clash was bound to happen.

I was exhausted when I got to the office that morning. The night before had been date night with hubby, and my brain was flying at half mast. I went in without any bright ideas about topics to discuss, but then content producer Denise Rapitsi raised the fact that it was Biko Day. I said, of course! I thought we could mention him: a struggle hero and the father of Black Consciousness.

From the blank stares of our head producer and my co-host, however, I knew I didn't have buy-in. This did not come as a surprise. I knew they wouldn't see what angle we could take on one of the most relevant days in South African history. Like Youth Day being the day we wear our old school uniforms and share high-school memories instead of discussing how the youth is moving the country forward today because of the brave actions of the young people of 1976.

And after the exhausting arguments we'd had before over content – because I clearly still lacked an understanding of who exactly Jacaranda's listeners were – I chose not to fight for the topic. But I made a mental note to slip Biko Day into the conversation. It might not matter to listeners, but it sure as hell mattered to me.

As with any other show, we'd sift through headlines, online and in print, to see if anything tickled our fancy. A couple of publications were running a story on Steve Hofmeyr, who had been banned from performing at certain venues overseas. Steve Hofmeyr, if you do not know him, is an Afrikaans musician. He is also hailed by his followers for fighting for the pride and interests of white South Africans. At some point he organised a march against white genocide called Red October. It was confusing for most; we knew that many South Africans were getting killed, but we were not aware that white people were leading the pack.

Hofmeyr has also said some extreme things, even going so far, in 2014, as to tweet that *black* people were the architects of apartheid. Those South Africans who have run away because they can't bear the idea of black leadership love having people like Steve to remind them why they must not come back. (I support that fully. If you can't love this place, stay away; it's a win-win.)

I figured any topic on that guy would have the listeners' ears tuned to me, not Martin, simply because, as a race, white people were out of bounds for me. At least, that is how I had been made to feel. I was, after all, where I 'did not belong'. And, in retrospect, I agree that I did not belong in the Steve Hofmeyr conversation. I figured, therefore, that this topic would be dismissed as quickly as it came up. Nope, not what happened. I did sound the alarm by saying that Steve Hofmeyr was a sensitive topic, and that we would have the right-wing extremists coming after us if we discussed him on air. I offered to sit back a bit.

I was also reticent about my standpoint on the matter. Even though I don't like Hofmeyr's views, I didn't quite understand why he had been banned. The man was going to sing, not lead a political rally; I hadn't realised that his politics had become an issue overseas. He would be performing with a couple of artists of colour, so it couldn't have been a KKK-level of show, surely. I decided that my safest position would be one of 'inquisitive bystander'. This was a case of one group of South Africans pitted against another. Black South Africa was the backdrop, but this issue, in my view, was a debate about representation. It would be, in heritage month, a discussion around people having a right to say what does and doesn't represent them.

I warned that it would get touchy, and everyone agreed that the direction the conversation went would be controlled. Our aim would be to find out who was behind the ban, and why. Also, because Hofmeyr had spoken before on behalf of a 'threatened minority', I wanted to know if he was planning another one of his smear campaigns against South Africans of colour. Done. The rest was none of my business.

To be fair, Jacaranda is a music and entertainment station; you don't want to bog it down with anything that requires critical thinking or too much introspection. Just good times. When Jacaranda hired me, they took on one of the most outspoken women in comedy – outspoken about race, politics, gender-based bullshit – but as a mouthpiece of the good times, my job, at that point, was to be a clown and a drawcard for those mommies who love the station. Beyond that, you park you. Well, at that moment, I parked me. But I did start scrolling through my phone for Biko quotes to throw out during the show.

So we went on air, and it was business as usual. Listeners were divided on the Hofmeyr issue. They stood either for or against him, they agreed strongly or strongly disagreed with him. There did not seem to be an in-between. It was fascinating. I enjoyed listening to the seemingly sensible people who argued for freedom of speech, but I started to lose my shit with the ones who were turning it into a 'fuck the blacks' conversation.

I began backing off, but the issue of representation was still open. What got me incensed, as the topic started veering in a tasteless direction (so much for control), was the flippancy with which apartheid was mentioned. Once again, it was implied that blacks refused to get past it. When we were on air, I would habitually check what was happening on the show's Facebook timeline so that I could alert the producer if anything came up that added to the talkability of the topic.

So, naturally, as this conversation unravelled I was glued to the show's Facebook timeline. It did not gradually swell and then explode; it simply erupted. The aggressive and defensive tone of the comments worried me. It was turning into a war of words between a minority who felt that Steve defended them in a land where they were targets, and people who agreed that he should not be given a platform to spread hate. Sadly, the louder voice was that of the mad minority.

Their comments did not make me angry, but they hurt, so I shared this Steve Biko quote from the biography *Cry Freedom* by Donald Woods:

'There is nothing to be ashamed of in language and culture. In fact you should be proud of these things!' I shared it because, despite our historical friction, I do not believe Afrikaners should be ashamed of who they are. As a culture and as a language, it is part of the heartbeat of this great nation of ours.

I said this long before I went on to speak about my view on race. I thought I had made it clear that I was not on the attack. I spoke honestly, because my blackness had been a reason for the almost constant stream of vitriol against me on social media. I did not know that my opinion could scare people to such an extent. Yet those same people had no problem airing their unpalatable views and expecting me to take it on the chin.

Well. I should have thought about the two factors that meant I should never have even taken part in that conversation if I wanted peace in my life: my race and my gender. Sure, my role as a host was to drive the story, but I was speaking to an audience that barely knew me but was acutely aware of my blackness. Add to that certain Afrikaans people's oversensitivity about their heritage and you can't even make a comment without them giving you a concise history of the Anglo-Boer war.

I was already in people's bad books because the well-meaning Barney Simon had played a clip of my comedy earlier that year during his radio slot. In the clip I talked about poor white beggars, and how much harder it was to accept that they existed than black beggars. Because of history, I said, black people have unofficially *owned* suffering in this country. I joked that I give a black beggar two rand, but a white beggar ten rand, because shame, they haven't had to survive much as a race. 'Black people, we survive. Slavery, we survived. Apartheid, we survived. What have white people survived? E-Tolls?'

The audience would always erupt with laughter at this. But oh no, not on Barney's show. Instead, I got long emails about the concentration camps that Afrikaners had been incarcerated in during the Anglo-Boer War. I got BCCSA complaints. I got a massive headache. I had a hunch then that I would not last long at Jacaranda.

In addition, unlike other people of colour at that station (in my opinion anyway), I wore my blackness blatantly, although I didn't deliberately plan on doing so. I was unapologetically bad at Afrikaans, but I spoke what I could with the intention of becoming as fluent as I was when I was younger and spoke it more often. I did not pretend to understand things around white culture that confused me. Rather, I made it a sort of cultural exchange: you teach me, I teach you. I was not there to pander to outdated thinking – I was there to take people with me on a journey of what South Africa really is: a melting pot of cultures that has no space for polarisation of black and white, non-Afrikaans-speaking and Afrikaans-speaking.

A listener once had the nerve to tell me which accent she preferred me to use. She did not like my more natural, harder black South African accents; she preferred my voice-over accent. My jaw dropped purely out of muscle memory. I have spent so much of my career (corporate gigs) around white people who reminded me of my blackness that I have become damn conscious of it; it has become a part of my language and humour. And I won't be apologising for that.

So, when some guy left a voice note on our show claiming that blacks bring up apartheid when it suits them, I kind of lost my mind. I mean, I am human; we all break at some point. I made it clear, before his comment, that every village must handle its own idiot. In other words, when people claiming to speak on your behalf lose the plot, call them out.

In response to the man's comment, I said that the black people who are still angry about apartheid are like a child who had his bike stolen by a bully on the playground. Then an adult intervened and, instead of dealing with the injustice done to the child, told the child to share his bicycle with the bully. Of course that child would feel angry and unjustly treated.

I knew this analogy would rattle cages, but I did not think it would lead to thousands of people coming after me, and the station, with such venom. I did not call any group of people bullies; I spoke about a system. I did not call for anyone to be punished, yet people sent me pictures of sick white babies and asked me if that was the 'punishment' they deserved. I mean, who does that?

I should have known from the way I trembled after relating the analogy how my life would change forever. I felt as if something was shifting in me; I couldn't understand why my senses were overreacting. Nevertheless, my nervous system decided to sound the fight-or-flight alarm, and my system defences started their engines in response, not quite sure whether to barricade or attack.

I mumbled, 'Why am I shaking?', but nobody responded. Martin didn't look me in the eye. I thought, *If my co-pilot isn't with me, I am screwed.* As we left the studio, we were expecting some of the usual *'sy is 'n rassis'* backlash, but nothing like the shit storm that followed.

Colour me ignorant, I only found out the next day exactly which of the things I'd said had so many people up in arms. One of them was when I called black people 'people of the soil', because apparently it implied that Afrikaners are *not* people of the soil. Then, they were angry because they said I'd called white people playground bullies and said they should be punished. (And yet those very people offended by this were bullying me on Facebook and Twitter. They even harassed my manager, thinking he was me.)

Forgive me, but I laughed at this. My response was, 'If the shoe fits.' But regarding retribution: if I say I am explaining why I am angry, and you respond by saying I am attacking you, then you were never interested in the reasons for my anger. I did not call for retribution or punishment, I only offered insight into people's feelings, so surely I cannot be accused of racism. But my narrative of that day was rewritten, and that is why I continue to feel uncomfortable around white strangers. I do not know which version they heard, and whether a crazy one will shoot or stab me because they believe I want *them* killed. How we got there, goodness knows. The experience was traumatic for me in ways I cannot articulate.

What I find most disturbing is how some Afrikaners have decided that apartheid is a part of who they are. You mention apartheid, and it is as if you said something about their mother, and when we condemn it, we condemn them. They seem to think that when we say that there was no real retribution for the atrocities of apartheid, it means we are asking for someone to be burnt at the stake. The same people are happy to hear you criticise black politicians, but you cannot say anything about theirs. You can put on a Leon Schuster black accent and they'll roll on the floor laughing, but speak like a 'boet' or a 'poppie' and they'll say, 'Don't speak the language if you are going to speak it like that.'

The first group to react to what I had said was the Afrikaans Christian trade union Solidariteit, who sent me a Twitter message to say they would be demanding a recording of the show. I wished them luck. Apparently, that incensed them even further. I mean, how deeply offended were people to send an entire AfriForum and Solidariteit army after me? Businesses threatened to pull their advertising, and some did.

Not long after Tumigate broke, we made a trip as a team to Mpumalanga on a rhino-saving outside broadcast. Someone spotted the Jacaranda vans and sent a message to a Facebook group that was boycotting our station. I was sent screen grabs of a group of social-media activists who had shared the location of the Jacaranda vehicles they had seen, pointing out that I must be there too. Everyone began to panic. It didn't scare me, perhaps because I knew I was dealing with cowards.

I was sent pictures of white people who had been gruesomely killed on farms, with the tag 'Is this the punishment you want for us?' A woman sent me a picture of a white baby with some kind of cancer and asked if that was the punishment Afrikaners deserved. There are some really sad, hollow souls out there, and they had all come out to play. But I refused to take part in this game. I did not respond. I simply deleted and blocked until it became so time-consuming that I could no longer go onto social media. It was also becoming emotionally exhausting to read all that ugliness. Everything I had ever said that had rubbed people the wrong way was twisted and thrown back at me. I just gave up. This was one fight I was not going to win. They needed someone to attack, and I was it.

I was warned to take my name off the car I was driving. At some point, my husband and my father-in-law wanted to take turns driving me to work so I wouldn't have to drive alone. The men in my life were more scared for me than I was for myself. All because the people who claimed I had called them bullies were now bullying me.

There were calls for my car sponsorship to be pulled, because Steve Hofmeyr's car sponsorship had been pulled after he was accused of racism. This was an eye for an eye as far as these aggrieved people were concerned; they were clearly still upset by what had been done to their hero. It should not have stung to be called racist, because I know myself, but it did. What added to the pain was feeling as if I was being abandoned by an audience with whom I was trying to grow.

I began receiving WhatsApp messages from friends and people in politics whom I had never spoken to in my life. I was told to stay away from social media and let someone else handle it. I was told to cut unnecessary communication, take preventative measures like using a different number, ditching my current car, and getting in touch with certain individuals who could provide protection. I thought everyone was overreacting – this storm would surely blow over soon?

However, it eventually became clear that the people on WhatsApp had a better idea of what was going on than I did. As a result of the rather precarious position I found myself in, I realised that I did not trust the people around me. I became paranoid; it was like being on a bad marijuana high.

Even some black folk scared me, with their response to the situation. I had not come across such burning hatred and anger towards white people except in movies I had seen about oppression. They were ready to take this fight to the streets. To go to Jacaranda. However, Jacaranda was not attacking me, although the station had issued a kind of Pontius Pilate statement, saying they supported my freedom of speech, but would follow due course if the BCCSA found fault with what I had said. I read it as noncommittal.

Then, when the fire did not die, I was allowed to finally have my say, by which time the issue was no longer in my hands. The journalists to whom I had not commented had drawn their own conclusions and printed their own stories. Then the issue became about hitting back at white people. I did not like the idea. The fringe was reaching out to me at this point, but I did not care which side of the fence they were on; I was not about to let anyone take control of the narrative to start a bigger race war.

Some folks showered me with love, offering me everything from protection to public declarations of support, which made me realise that I should hold on to my perception of what South Africans are: a united front with a few broken links. I was told to hang in there. I was offered prayer. A church in Cape Town offered to fly me over so that we could deal with the pain of the past together.

I was touched but confused, because it also felt a little like a trap. Look, I was paranoid, despite the fact that I enjoyed the genuine conversations and debates regarding where we are as a country that resulted from the furore. I also enjoyed the break from social media when I finally decided to heed the advice and delete all my social-media apps.

In all of this I channelled Mama and her ability to get through troubled times with a sense of humour and her head held high. So I would pretend to be in stealth mode when I left the house and interacted with colleagues at work. I jokingly asked if it would be better if I rode a bicycle to work so my critics could see that I'd got the bicycle back and that everything was okay now. I even offered to record a mixed-race sex tape so that I could traumatise everyone into forgetting about the comment. Bad jokes, but they amused me and made me feel better.

Meanwhile, Bonsu fell gravely ill. He had missed school because of a tight chest, but the next day he was weak and struggling to breathe. When he turned blue, he was rushed to the emergency ward. By the time I reached him, he was hooked up to an oxygen tank and to a drip filled with steroids to keep his lungs open. The world around me stopped. While a witch-hunt was out for a black bitch who dared express herself on other people's radio, a mother was scared for her son. I kept getting threatening messages, social media was an inferno and calls from journalists were streaming in by the hour, but I had to keep a low profile and be there for my child. At the same time, I had to stay on air. I did all of that – and I made the trip to Mpumalanga to save some rhinos. Shit. Was. Real.

Before the Mpumalanga trip, I spent a couple of nights at the hospital with my boy. The doctor was still trying to figure out what was wrong with him. As I sat there, a white boy was brought in. He was in terrible pain, and quite distressed. Bonsu told me that it was the boy who had bullied him in school a while back. It had got so bad that Mpho approached the school, and they had dealt with the bully.

And now here he was, sharing a ward with my son. I wept for the first time since Tumigate broke. Bonsu asked me to help him out of bed, then shuffled over to this boy, wheeling his oxygen and drip along, and offered the kid his fidget spinner. It felt too damn serendipitous, even for the universe, to see this kind of compassion with everything that was going on around me.

I became an emotional wreck at this point. I probably aged a whole five years during that Jacaranda saga. I then had to go to the hospital chemist to get medicine for Afia, who is a seasonal asthmatic. She had begun displaying the same symptoms as her brother and her paediatrician was aggressively medicating her before her condition could deteriorate. I prayed she would not be hospitalised too; we had already been through that earlier in the year.

While I was at the chemist, some dishevelled white guy came to the counter with cuts and bruises. I avoided eye contact at all times so that I wouldn't be recognised and engaged in a discussion about what was happening, but this guy made eye contact. I looked away quickly, pretending to stare at my phone. When I looked up again, he was looking at me, phone in hand. Panic rose. Was he about to take a picture of me and send it to his people? Would they storm the hospital? My heart tried to escape my body and save itself. Before I could decide my next move, I was called to the counter. A kind of defiance began to envelop me. I cleared my throat and got on with my business. If shit was going to hit the fan here, so be it. At least medical emergency staff would be at hand. So would witnesses and surveillance cameras.

I am not a racist. Out there, though, are people perpetuating the story that I am, because they feel threatened. They do not like what I said in jest, or what I said in seriousness. Since they are mostly male, I am assuming it is because they also don't take kindly to a woman who speaks 'out of turn'. They certainly do not like anyone who challenges their view that they themselves are victims in some kind of imagined danger.

It took me a while, but I am okay with that. It hurt a lot when I first had to deal with being called a racist. Mainly because I had to sit and ask myself if the assumption was correct and I had been spewing racist bile unconsciously. It is ironic, though, how many old South African flags featured on the profile pages of the people who were calling *me* a racist; it helped to take the sting out.

Am I bitter about what happened? Damn right I am. I am still fucking furious when I think about it. I am mad because I tried to level the playing field by speaking as an equal in what I thought was an adult conversation. I was in this thing for a two-sided debate, not to open myself to attack or provoke anyone.

I am mad because I had sensed the danger of having this conversation in the first place, and mad because I knew commenting would lead to a point of no return. I wish I had insisted that they leave me out of this one. I am mad because it feels like absolute bullshit that we must still deal with this kind of backward conversation in this day and age. I am mad at the irony that I was bullied. Mad because I did not realise my own power until I had stepped away from the situation.

Then I took a quick left turn to the realisation that this was not about me. This was about a station that was perceived to belong to a group of people, and those people feeling like they were losing their grip on it. And when that threat acquired a face, a black female face, a soft target was born. Suddenly these people had something to wake up for. Something to shoot at, to attack, to take down, as a symbol of an imagined institution that employed apartheid tactics to denigrate and disempower white South Africans, particularly Afrikaners.

If I wasn't so busy raising a family and making my million, I would have risen to the challenge of facing this Goliath. I am no Mandela. My patience runs thinner than Donald Trump's hair, and I can only handle so much policing before I go rogue. I spent every day after that incident feeling as if I were fighting with myself. I thought, any other deejay would have been allowed to fight this out on air somehow – whether directly or indirectly. It's not even about Jacaranda, it's about this country. It is about how easy it is to lose your agency and your voice as a woman. Add your skin colour to that and your troubles are twofold.

Never before have I been talked down to and talked at to such an extent. And this thing lasted, at most, two months. Then it reared its ugly head again when I was targeted that November over a harmless roast. Let me tell you, my friend, you wanna make kak with people who will *take you down*, start kak with right-wing Afrikaners.

I got tired of sifting through their exhausting, juvenile responses and decided that there were more important things to do, like figuring out creative ways to post about my experiences with the sponsored Jaguar F-Pace I had the joy of driving for the year. Oh yeah, that's another thing that irked them: I was too successful, in their eyes. And they couldn't stand it. It is sad, man, people who live in this mentality of victimhood and lack, trapped in their own ignorance, unwilling to consider change.

After the outbreak of fire and brimstone, I was invited to a sit-down with AfriForum. I was even invited to go to the Voortrekker Monument. (I was in high school in the late nineties – there is nothing new you can teach me about that monument. I got a B for history in matric and it featured in my essay.) For all the bad taste the AfriForum meeting left in my mouth – I was expected to go through with it – it was probably the most insightful meeting of my adult life. And I do not say that lightly.

It was as uncomfortable as having to hand over the whip that will be used to give you a hiding. But even in my own convictions I have always tried to be open to paradigm shifts, to perspectives that I may have missed. I was worried, though, that if these people wanted to make an example of me, it could result in a bloodbath, so I put together a 'dream team' delegation to join me.

Although AfriForum had not asked that Martin join us, I insisted that he be a part of my delegation. I asked for our then producer, Denise Rapitsi, to be there, because I did not want to feel like the token black woman from the station, and I said as much. I also requested the presence of Mighti Jamie, a great legal mind with impressive socio-political know-how. He was diplomatic, and I liked his style.

Without discussing it with me, my bosses replaced Denise with our white producer. At least I got Mighti. Without him, I would have felt like the naughty black who had been brought in to be disciplined in an intervention by well-meaning white people. I could have chosen to get mad, but I had bigger fish to fry.

I was about to face the so-called representatives of white Afrikaans South Africa, and I did not know enough about them; I just knew I regarded them with the same trepidation as I did the right-wing AWB. The face of the deeply aggrieved and offended. The *baas* was ready to sit the little black girl down and get her to toe the line.

I needed to shift this narrative. People often act with a lack of perspective when they come face to face with others who are not a part of their 'normal' lives. In other words, white dudes who do not interact with black women other than their domestics will not know how to deal with a high-flying black executive outside of an office setting. They have not taken enough interest to engage the humans behind the work titles, and therefore do not understand us. Pigeon-holing is easy when you see people as standard-issue racial stereotypes instead of three-dimensional beings. Here's my size four-and-a-half shoe; just slip it on for a moment.

I was raised to respect my elders. So in any conflict, the elder starts with a one-point lead, because I will humble myself in respect for their age. Then, men. I grew up without my father from the age of six, and I never again had a constant father figure in my life. Men have hurt and subjected me, so I approach them with caution. Race, on the other hand, has never been an issue in my interpersonal relationships, but it was the whole reason for this meeting.

A tsunami of hate was coming at me from some white people. I felt they were ganging up on me. And now, at my most vulnerable, I was being robbed of the visual comfort of more colour in the room. The over-representation of whiteness gave me the impression that this would be a meeting in which I would be exhibit A and the others would debate among themselves, and that would be that. It felt like an out-of-body experience. Rian termed it 'the koeksister meeting', because we enjoyed the traditional Afrikaans dessert during our little get-together.

I cannot speak for the intentions of my well-meaning colleagues; I can only speak for what I saw at this 'koeksister meeting', which I had tried to decline. Three phone calls and a conference call later, after being told the ball was still in my court, I knew I did not want to take part in it. And yet here I was, being a team player.

Unfortunately, I cannot share what happened in that room – we all agreed not to divulge the events of that day. But I can tell you this: I walked away more convinced than ever that this had not been about me. It was about perception and the need to assert power. I wondered why anyone would think that I am not familiar with South African history, or assume that I speak from a place of ignorance when a sensitive topic like race is broached. Nothing like an educated black woman to mess with your reality.

I have a recurring nightmare when I am under stress. In this nightmare I confront the people who hurt me as a child. I begin to tell them how I really feel, but my nose and throat close up and, as I start suffocating, my heart races and nobody can help me. When I decide to give in to death, I wake up. I only have these dreams when people have hurt or offended me and I have left the issue unresolved. I did not have them during Tumigate. That was my first win.

During the writing of this book, Lucas Manyane Mangope passed away. I called my father. Mangope, in my eight-year-old mind, had been sym-bolic of everything that tore my family apart.

I felt quite emotional after the news broke. I was at the radio station at the time, and never had I wished more to be on a different radio platform than at that moment, when I wanted to talk about what it was like to grow up in Bophuthatswana. It was a bitter pill to swallow, seeing how this monster was now being glorified on social media.

The first thing I asked my father was whether he had forgiven Mangope. His answer was lengthy, but I summarised it as a yes. Then he paused, and said, 'All my enemies are now dead. I only ever had two enemies in my life: Seleke and Mangope.' He told me how P.J. Seleke had threatened him, telling my father he would die in a car accident while driving the government-issue car he was given as a cop. Instead, Seleke died in a nasty car crash some years later. And now Mangope was gone, too.

In measured words and emotions, my father told me, once again, how he had lost both his parents and could not bury them. (Yet Oscar Pistorius gets to go to family funerals ... Must be nice.) My father was broken by his mother's death, and by the time the news of his father's came months later, there was nothing left to break. All he could do was walk back to his cell and share the news with his cadres. His report-back was so matter-of-fact that they did not believe him at first.

I thought back to the white people who had questioned my right to be angry about apartheid. How do they get to decide the measure of anyone's pain or experiences? I listened to that breakfast show again and still failed to understand how I had incited hate. In its ruling, the BCCSA recommended that we tread carefully when talking about race. I have attributed the fallout to the immediacy and intimacy of radio. The feedback on other, unrelated conversations on air was that I sounded aggressive, even when I was clearly taking the mickey.

Being polite didn't help. Stepping back and allowing the aggrieved few to vent did not help either. I am nobody's dumping ground, and the level of abuse I have had to endure did not even match the alleged crime. I was in a space where I had to accommodate a few faceless people whose toes I dared not step on. My reality was too challenging for them – I was on their territory, but I still had an issue with the unsavoury part of our country's history. I felt oppressed and angry, even though I live in a free world where I am part of the majority and it is now my turn to speak.

Then Hugh Masekela died, and I could not even pay homage to the role his music had played in our emancipation, telling the stories of our pain, our struggle and his undying love for his country. No, because when the word apartheid comes out of my mouth, it is seen as a declaration of war. I am telling you, being in a place where you feel like the elephant in the room can give you a major complex. I consciously need to remind myself to rise above the anger.

As for Mangope, well … I am sorry for his family's loss, but I hope they know what kind of man this so-called visionary was as well. I acknowledge the infrastructure and legacy he left as much as the lives he destroyed to build those things. There are people who lost their land, their livelihood, their lives in order for him to fulfil this 'vision' for which he is now praised.

Mama always said that I talk too much, and perhaps I have said too much on this issue. But it has to be said. I struggle to make sense of racism. A hunger for power, delusions of grandeur, a need to divide and conquer – those things make sense to me. They are easier enemies to defeat. Racism is smoke and mirrors: it distracts you from the real issues.

When a black man is willing to sell out his own people in a system where even he himself was considered a dog, you can't just be angry at a single race; you must be angry at all the cogs in that wheel. If you happen to be one of the white Afrikaners who labelled me a racist, I trust that, by this point, you see that I am not angry at a specific race.

Actually, I don't care whether you get it or not – I am telling you. I'll say it again – and it may keep coming up in this book: *fuck apartheid.*

10

Mona ha se ha 'buru le shweleng

(*This is not a dead Boer's house*)

Whenever we were making too much noise, or were fighting or acting in an untoward manner, Mama would shout: *'Mona ha se ha 'buru le shweleng!'* (This is not a dead Boer's house!) As long as Mama was there as a figure of authority, I would toe the line. Mind you, by 'there' I mean, alive. Even when she wasn't watching, I had to be exemplary. If she came home after a weekend away and found her house a mess, I would get the dead-Boer lecture.

I left Jacaranda FM in March 2018. After I left, my friends and family suddenly came clean about how they really felt about the station and the fact that I was working there. Most of them knew about my bucket-list wish of going on radio, and my stint at CliffCentral had made sense to them. I had used that experience to gain online radio experience, but I wanted to make a move to traditional radio and, well, they figured I would be aiming at talk radio. They envisioned a Eusebius McKaiser-esque scenario, less well-read but certain to cause waves. For them, Jacaranda was an unsolved puzzle. Their puzzlement left me puzzled, and I wondered if it would be my Will Smith *Matrix* moment – he had chosen to star in *Wild Wild West* rather than playing Neo in *The Matrix*. The latter became a massive hit, while *Wild Wild West* tanked, hard. I chose Jacaranda over a tour and two television opportunities. I loved radio; it was sexy, uncharted territory. It wasn't for the money – I would not have gone into it in that case. I just wanted to try my hand at it.

Even today, I don't resent Jacaranda; I just realised too late that it was not the right space for me. What shocked me, however, was how some of my friends, associates and family reacted once I'd left the station. Ex-DJs and other people who had crossed paths with Jacaranda said to me, 'When I heard you were going to that place, I wished you had spoken to me first.'

My friends were relieved that I had decided to leave. Apparently I was changing, and not in a good way. According to them, I was becoming a watered-down version of the girl they knew. It was rather obvious, too. I was putting on weight, my skin was breaking out and I was doubting myself more than I had when I'd first started out in entertainment. I was colouring inside the lines too much and not playing as much as I used to. *How did I get here*, I wondered?

Perhaps it was the faith I had in being able to connect with people, a faith I had learnt from my mother. Mama was loved and lovable because she loved people. I think I inherited that from her. What I did not inherit, however, was the ease with which she engaged with people before they engaged with her. The only time I manage that with any confidence is when I am safely behind a microphone, in full performance mode.

In fact, people intimidate the hell out of me. My first assumption is always the worst. I am so afraid of rejection or reproach that I give people a wide berth until I see some kind of physical sign that they are interested in interacting with me. I know it sounds like hogwash because I am a performer, but it is the truth. The cool thing about performance is that there is a healthy distance between me and the audience and my status is already established.

Offstage, I fear being eaten alive. It is one of my most illogical fears and I hate it. Seriously, I would make a terrible Jehovah's Witness, because I would never have the guts to knock on someone's door. But once you have let the brave knocker in, I'd step forward and *nail* the sales pitch. That's the thing: once I am in, I am in, and I go *all* in. You would be 'saved' in no time and happily give up Valentine's Day, birthdays and Christmas forever.

This has been my narrative, even going into Jacaranda. I was so afraid of entering that space, but I was enticed by the idea that once I had read the audience, I could bring them over to the Tumi side of things. I thought, *There is no reason why I can't settle here. I am good enough and there is no law that says I can't.*

Mama's car once broke down on our way to Thaba Nchu from Mafikeng. We were a little distance away from a farmstead, Afrikaans-owned, of course. My nanny fearfully suggested that we wait for help or walk until we hit a town. Mama said no; she will *praat* the *taal* and get the farmer to help; he was right there, after all. She didn't even need to make the trip, as the guy had already noticed how long the car had been there and had made his way to us in his van.

Mama put on her biggest smile, tilted her head and spoke Afrikaans in the humblest tone. She was such a charmer, that one! No wonder they called her white bread. The farmer, who had started off quite gruffly, sounded less and less hostile as the conversation continued, and by the end of it he and Mama were both laughing. Together they checked under the car's bonnet and, well, we made it to Thaba Nchu safe and sound.

I figured, as Mama's daughter, that that could be my Jaca journey. I'd start out as a perceived threat of some sort, and then become the friend you want to spend a little time with every day – someone who isn't there to take anything away from you.

Before I joined the station, I had been on Jacaranda a couple of times. The first time was in 2014, after the Steve Hofmeyr Roast (which, incidentally was the first and only time I met the man in person. He seemed like a decent enough human being.). I was then invited back a couple of times, and each time the response was fantastic. So one day, after an interview on Rian van Heerden's breakfast show, I was asked to have a sit-down with programme manager Gavin Meiring, who wanted to gauge my interest in radio and whether I would be willing to do a show on Jacaranda.

We talked about my training, what I was up to at the time, and how I was definitely interested in radio. At the time I had a show on CliffCentral called *Sipping Tea*; I was using that show to gain some online radio experience and learn about running desks, etc. The big difference between online and on air, in my view, is that online, anything goes. You are uncensored. You break all traditional radio decorum and let the nature of the show and the host dictate what goes. No BCCSA to answer to, as the presenters on traditional radio have to do. No gatekeeper to keep you in check. Gavin thought I had a cool rapport on air and the listeners always gave positive feedback when I visited the station. I thought this was great. I figured I could do a graveyard shift, perhaps get to know the place first and then see what happened.

A few months later, I met with Gavin and station manager Kevin Fine, at the Marble Bar in Rosebank. Kevin came across as slightly edgy and seemed to lack a sense of humour, but he was genuinely interested in having me join the station. I was not sure why, though. He did not seem to be familiar with me or my work. But I went with the flow; maybe Gavin could keep him up to speed. When they left, I got on the phone with my agent, Osman. He was sceptical, and we scheduled a meeting of our own.

Osman could not understand why I wanted to do this, but was willing to hear me out. I explained that I wanted to increase my base, and my last one-man show had had a healthy multiracial audience, so I figured I could tap further into this market. I had been gigging in Pretoria, Centurion, the East Rand, the Free State and at golf-days packed with middle-aged Afrikaans-speakers, and it had all gone swimmingly. It seemed a natural progression to connect with more of those people and increase bums on seats. So that is how I sold the idea to Osman, who then backed me and agreed to help make it happen.

And so I joined Jacaranda, and with it some people whose company I enjoyed both inside and outside the workplace. A little undervalued, that talent at Jacaranda; maybe even they do not know their worth. Those studios in Midrand make radio look so cool. The walls consist of murals of international and local music stars. There are tag lines along the corridor – 'Lekker to be here', 'More music you love'. The holding areas are impressive, and you receive a warm reception from everyone you come across, as if they are hosting you themselves.

However, in the background there was a certain lack of straightforwardness that bothered me. Jacaranda had approached another presenter before me, so clearly I was plan B or C. I recorded demos with two different DJs, and I had to keep checking if I was in the running. In retrospect, I should have maybe backed out at that point.

Eventually, I was told that they had decided on the perfect match for me: Martin Bester. I had heard of him; I loved his cheekiness in the afternoon slot. I agreed that our partnership would work like a charm, and it turned out that our common interests went even deeper: we share the same birthday, seven years apart. In the meantime, I would be on air with Mack Rapapali on weekends to familiarise myself with being on the airwaves. I enjoyed it so much that I even asked Gavin if we couldn't make this my entry into the station. He, presenter-slash-comedy-stuntman MalJan and I enjoyed a lot of laughter and feel-good vibes. Alas, that was not part of the big plan.

Jacaranda and I were a beautiful love story waiting to happen. Pity it ended as a Greek tragedy.

Before Martin and I went on air, we spent a couple of months playing around with content, deciding on what we enjoyed talking about. I wasn't joining the radio station to be a clown; I was joining, I thought, to be a comical sidekick to the main guy. I figured that my name was in the title of the show to entice new listeners. It made sense, as Martin is also a funny guy, although not a comedian. Excellent wit, tongue-in-cheek. He would push the envelope a bit, and I would push it a little further. I tried to play it safe, though; or at least I thought I did. My intention was clear: to help the audience to get to know me by speaking as a mom and a wife. I wanted to let the comedy come naturally. I was in a new space, a new medium, so I wanted to take my time.

My husband will tell you that I hate waking up early. If sleeping in were a religion, I would be a faithful congregant. When I told Mpho that I was joining breakfast radio, he raised an eyebrow. Really? I agreed to *that*? Well, then, I would have to practise waking up early in the months leading up to the gig. I am *not* a morning person, and Mpho pitied my poor colleagues. While he had a chuckle, I had a minor freak-out.

What the hell did I just get myself into? I pride myself on being the person who always shows up, though. Throughout bereavements and emotionally challenging times, I always showed up for work. I gave it my all and did not make my problems anyone else's. At those times, Tumi Morake took over and locked Mrs Osei-Tutu away until the job was done. I became so good at this that it became a habit, even when I wasn't working.

Brave fronts are my thing. When my mother passed away, the first thing I did when I got back from the funeral the following week was to jump on stage at Comedy Underground; it was just the therapy I needed. After my grandmother's passing, I was forced to show up for work when Whacked Agency refused to take me off a Cape Town line-up. They became less like my management and more like the bosses from hell. After an argument over the phone, we settled on a compromise: I would be at my grandmother's place in Thaba Nchu for the week, return to Johannesburg on the Thursday to catch a flight to Cape Town, do the first performance on the Friday line-up, then rush to catch the last flight out to Johannesburg. I'd land in Johannesburg, drive down to Thaba Nchu to make the funeral, and take the next flight out to perform again that evening.

My grandmother had raised me, and we were close, yet I arrived at her funeral feeling like a stranger, and I left soon after as one. I was hardened, wearing my game face; the show must go on, after all. I resented my management for putting me through the ordeal. Three close family members had died in the space of one year, and the people tasked with taking care of me were treating me like nothing more than a cash cow.

And I had allowed it to happen. I had stopped valuing myself. I was stuck on the runaway train that was Tumi Morake, and I did not know how to get off. I sank into a depression, missing every warning sign along the way. Mpho could see I was unhappy, but I bit his head off every time he brought it up. I did not want to have to admit that I wasn't coping as well as I was pretending to. This was my chosen path, that of a performer. I needed to show up and kick ass, and I would do the same at Jacaranda.

I had made a mental note of all the factors that could work against me – loud, un-PC, unapologetically, smartass black. Yeah, I do not subscribe to the safe black game. I did not step into that space and assume that my presence on such a big show would be received with open arms. I had observed how Jacaranda's on-air personalities tread well within the rainbow, either consciously or unconsciously parking their identities to maintain the auditory comfort of their listeners. I respected that, but if I was at Jacaranda because of the kind of entertainer I was, I could not toe that line. My entertainment value is intertwined with my need to challenge, speak out and speak truth from a place of comedy.

However, Anele Mdoda (whom I consider a South African Oprah) warned me way up front that radio would change me. I will forever remember her sage words: 'Who you are on air and who you are out here will not be the same, and you will have to get used to that.' I should have heeded her words and perhaps been less resistant to the mindshift. Maybe I would still be at Jacaranda now, saving the world one Good Morning Angel at a time and chatting animatedly about a world I do not live in but, for three hours, could pretend to be a part of.

I am still not sure where things really went awry. I don't know when my rainbow-nation radio dream became a nightmare South African reality. We had promised to keep it real on this show. It got real, all right; too real, until it was really shitty.

Life seems to throw me into situations that remind me that I need to fly freely and express myself. I married a man from a conservative Catholic background, thereby entering into a union and a belief system that is notorious for clipping wings. I was raised in a household that reins in its children, and when I stood up to an aggressive relative and the authority that protected him, it took fifteen years to repair that relationship. Broadcasting is a hell of a balancing act between keeping the energy flowing and staying within its conservative boundaries.

Breakfast with Martin Bester and Tumi Morake had young fans, mommy fans and general adult fans. I got hate mail too, but that seemed to be gradually decreasing. Although my personal fan page was generating an unusual amount of hate mail, mostly telling me that I was horrible or that I should find a black radio station and leave this one alone, I could take it. Fan mail, even hate mail, meant people were listening. Over time the messages from people who liked the new show and enjoyed its light-heartedness increased. I was enjoying learning a gentler way of reaching out to people. Radio presented a new level of intimacy.

In the background, there was pressure to help the show gain traction, as with any new show, in particular one that replaces a popular host who had been in that slot for years. We had taken over from Rian van Heerden and were feeling the pressure, but pushing on. I sometimes feel, though, that we were done a disservice; the listeners were not told explicitly that Rian would be returning in a new slot. Some of them were resisting change quite audibly, so when Rian did return, they misread it as a sign of their influence.

We trudged on, but the team was slowly unravelling – there was a clash of personalities, with hangovers from the previous show. I am so used to working solo that this did not affect me much, at least initially. How I got sucked into it can be ascribed to human nature. Our team gradually changed – out of the core team of seven, only three of the original team would remain by the time I left. If that is not a sign that something isn't quite right, I don't know.

I played on the desk in my free time, because I was keen to learn how to run a show. I have never started anything without the intention of learning to master it, and radio is still one of those things. What I had enjoyed the most about Rian's show was that he presented the perfect balance of touching on the things that make South Africa tick, challenging listeners and being downright funny. Yes, I cringed sometimes, but I kept going back for more. I had hoped that we could maintain some of the best of that smart but entertaining content. Or have content where we would talk on a serious level, but then allow for a retrospective laugh.

Again, how naive. I had not considered how inept I was in under-standing the make-up of the station, nestled as it was in the *platteland*. I had not considered the reality that people don't always put their money where their mouths are. Jacaranda said they wanted to be socially pro-gressive, but they did not follow through. They wanted to hire a black woman in a prime-time slot to appear more diverse. In theory, they may have known that it would cost them some of their more conservative and right-leaning listeners, but they were willing to take the chance because the audience they would gain would eclipse the loss.

Unfortunately, from where I stood, they seemed to be in a constant state of two steps forward and ten steps back. I genuinely believed that Jacaranda wanted to reflect the South Africa that I know and love – multi-cultural, multilingual, with pain from the past but excitement about the future. Martin and I were so different, and as a writer, I know how much material comes from people finding commonality in seemingly different worlds. There is also the comedy of difference, when worlds are presented as polar opposites.

This, I think, is where all the trouble started. When I am in a mixed-race space, I own my blackness, because not to do so is to allow the other person to decide what they want to do with it. An example was when we decided to talk about funerals, because I had just returned from one in

Thaba Nchu and had shared my experiences with the team. The African approach to funerals is very different from the Western approach to funerals, and I thought we could extract some dark comedy out of it. The team that agreed on this topic was diverse, so if there were red flags we would have addressed them.

We went on air and joked about the one thing both types of funerals have in common: the people who are there only for the food. But I got into trouble for highlighting, in a funny way, the different ways in which we mourn. Our black mothers and aunts lose it completely, wailing, throwing themselves about, fainting. I compared it to the more controlled, quiet weeping at white funerals. Plus the sandwiches and platters served at white funerals, as opposed to the slaughtering of the beast and the giant three-legged pots at African funerals.

A complaint was made to the BCCSA claiming that I had said white people lack emotion. I was confused. If anyone should have been offended, it should have been the people I'd accused of putting on a mourning performance. Perhaps the problem was that it was the black girl poking fun at white people? It seems as if there is a small group of people who thrive on feeling victimised and will stop at nothing to have their victimhood confirmed. If I wasn't too loud for them, I was too offensive. People called in to support us, but no, I was still accused of attacking white people and saying that they have no feelings.

I should have known that this would be child's play compared to what would follow. Following this, the producer became safer and safer in the content she allowed, almost relegating me to the position of clown. I was given less to say, and became more of a soundboard than a thought leader. It began to feel more like *Breakfast with Martin Bester featuring Tumi Morake.*

I was asked to bring in more punchlines. I began to second-guess myself, to question whether I was actually getting this radio thing right. It was such an about-turn from being asked to sell my mom angle. I was getting frustrated, but I was learning. So I remained patient, believing there would be a pay-off in the future. Race was a non-issue for the most part. The issue was what makes good radio conversation.

Before the Tumigate fallout, I wanted to be there. I never met anyone half-assed about their job at Jacaranda. It is a well-oiled machine on that front, with a powerful culture. The staff will band together and make anything happen – it is almost an offence if you do not ask for help when you need it, and when work needs to be done, it gets done.

But I hate being policed, and when Tumigate broke, I was already feeling the restraint: I was too loud and had to quiet down; I was too brash and had to soften up – or mommy up; I was too comedy and had to be more real. So I became real, and stuck to the perspective of a mom, a wife. A working woman.

After Tumigate broke, I was told that I was not delivering *enough* comedy, and was made a suggestion that offended me deeply. The content producer told me about an old DJ who used to tell internet jokes, and asked me to do the same. *Me*. Tumi Morake, a reputable stand-up comedian, was asked to tell knock-knock-level jokes on radio. I honestly do not know how I would have looked at myself in the mirror, let alone face my comedy peers, if I did that to myself. It was referred to as my 'moment to shine'.

That hurt. Over ten years in comedy and public speaking, awarded in many respects, and here I was, being given a 'moment to shine' by telling jokes off the internet. I realised then that I had a bigger problem at this station than upsetting people by mentioning apartheid or commenting on whiteness. Clearly, I was the wrong fit. I wasn't whatever Jacaranda had imagined I would be. Instead, based on the hate mail, I seemed to be something their listeners feared.

I was in love with the craft of radio presenting, but I was beginning to hate the environment I was working in. Jacaranda might have wanted to support me, but at the same time they did not want to alienate their listeners. They seemed nervous that I would say something else that would cause an uproar. I was tired of it. When I began to be treated like a laugh track and a one-line commentator with a 'moment to shine', telling internet jokes, I switched off. Literally.

The sand was running out of the hourglass, and fast. All that time doing dry runs started to feel pointless. Going to work became just an opportunity to catch up on social media and play *Candy Crush*. My presence no longer had meaning. I felt like I was only there to save face, to win on principle.

Not everyone at Jacaranda was against me. Some of the staff told me that they fully supported me. The sense I got was that they genuinely cared and believed our collaboration could work. Come 2018, they were asking me why they weren't hearing me on air anymore. But I had checked out. I had been told in no uncertain terms that even though we had a social responsibility to this country, this was a music and entertainment station first and foremost. I was in safe-black zone, but I did not know when I had been spicy. Rian brought the most interesting politicians and thought leaders onto his show, but somehow our show was too spicy to handle such. There was no way I was going to survive permanent frivolity.

I wasn't even looking to have deep debates. While I was on sick leave, the H&M saga broke. H&M put out an advert featuring a little black boy in a hoodie with 'The coolest monkey in the jungle' written across it. Twitter went crazy. It was news headlines for a while.

I reckoned there was no way it would be discussed on the breakfast show, since music and entertainment were our mandate. Well, I nearly fell out of bed when the topic was broached. I was so touched, I switched to another station. I concluded, then, that *I* was the problem. My perspective was perhaps too black or too me (see what I did there?). Also, listening to this show, I realised it wouldn't miss me at all.

My ego could not bear it. I am *not* background noise. I did not come this far in life to be relegated to the background. The Tumi Morake brand did not match what this place was bending it into. As a person I am happy to blend in, but as Tumi Morake, my job is to stand out. Jacaranda didn't want me; it just wanted my name.

I take sage advice from my son Bonsu, who is an old soul. A couple of weeks after our Jaguar accident (more on that in the next chapter), he asked me if people at Jacaranda would be nicer to me now that they knew I'd been in an accident. It broke my heart. It had not been Jacaranda attacking me, and it was not Jacaranda that had to back off. Bonsu did not see it that way, and I felt like I had failed at protecting him from the ugliness. But I could still teach by example in how I dealt with it. I told him that there were mean people out there, but that there were even more people who were standing up for what was right.

But he gave me another talk that made me rethink my stay at Jacaranda when I was back home recovering from the accident. I has just been back at Jacaranda for a week after the crash when I had to take another week off because I was not coping with the pain. Bonsu came into my bedroom, and said he wanted to talk to me. Usually when he wants to talk it is either about something really deep, like when he asked to go and live with his grandparents because he was tired of fighting with his siblings (he got over that phase quickly, thank goodness), or it is purely about something silly. I always humour him, because of the entertainment value. This time, he seemed pretty serious. He said he had been thinking about me and thought I was not happy.

He said, 'You are this person, Mom, this really fun person, you know, like, you know, Mom. You. Okay, okay what I am saying is, Mom, Jacaranda takes that away from you. That's why I think you should leave. Then you can be you again.'

We hugged. He ran off. The waterworks again. I felt like someone old and wise was speaking to me through this child. I had to pay attention. If ever there was a neon sign pointing to the door, that was it. Since he began to speak in full sentences, Bonsu has floored me in those moments when he speaks like an old, wise man. When he was four, he called me 'a diamond in the laff' (he couldn't say his r's, so 'rough' became 'laff'). In Grade R I told him I wished I was a kid again so I could enjoy school as much as he did, and he said, 'You only go through this world but once.' So, yes, I take him seriously.

I asked for a meeting with Kevin Fine and told him I could not see myself spending another year with Jacaranda, and that I had no intention of renewing my contract in July. I was met with resistance. Kevin was honest. He knew what I had been through, but felt I would be letting the haters win if I left. I did not quite see it that way.

The haters were not my only problem: I did not like my work environment and it was draining me emotionally. I was underused and felt like a prop nobody knew quite how to handle. I am many things, but a prop? I have too strong a personality to be that. There are people who are happy to pick up a cheque at the end of the month for merely turning up, but I was not making the kind of money to justify that. Worst of all, I had reached a creative dead end.

We agreed that I would take a week to clear my head, and even consider taking extended leave so that I could return refreshed and mentally strong enough to carry on. In the end it was a tough decision, but I had to go. I was exhausted and I was unhappy. With such a lot on my plate, the easiest thing for me to offload was the last thing I had saddled myself with: radio. We had tried to make it work, but it was not serving me.

Bonsu asked me if I was going to accept any new radio offers. I said I was off radio for life, and he cried, 'But we need the money!' Funny kid.

'Am I not busy enough?' I asked.

He thought for a moment, as if pondering an important thing, and said, 'Yeah, actually you need to slow down.'

Yeah. I needed to find a steady running pace before I looked up and my babies were getting married and jetting off to distant lands.

There had been a bit of speculation about my 'real' reason for leaving Jacaranda FM. I kept getting asked about it, with people digging for subtext. Funny enough, I left for all the reasons I have shared either officially or unofficially. I left to spend more time with my family. I left because my children are still small and they need me. I left because I had bitten off more of a workload than I could chew. I left because I was uncomfortable with the idea of this cowardly bunch of racists targeting me, waiting to twist everything I said into a personal attack.

I left because I did not feel like there was enough buy-in to aggressively take the station in a new direction, and you cannot go on a one-man crusade to change things. The rainbow dream Jacaranda had sold me turned out to be fake. I left because I should not have been asked to redeem myself if we'd agreed that I had done nothing wrong. I left because I had to refuse a lot of exciting, lucrative prospects because of my commitment to the station.

Above all, I left because I cannot be caged. This seemingly white radio station, owned by a black holding company, just did not have a black enough agenda for me to stay.

Anele Mdoda invited me on her show, *Real Talk with Anele*, to discuss cyber-bullying and weathering social-media storms. Nobody knew about the resignation yet, so I figured appearing on the show wouldn't compromise me or the station. I agreed because Anele's a friend with a talk show and, come on, she's *Anele*, but also because the topic under discussion was something I really felt was not discussed enough from the perspective of people who live in the public eye and have to wade through those murky waters on a daily basis.

However, my PR team and I failed to anticipate the paranoia of someone who knew I was leaving Jacaranda and thought I was running to 947 to rally against Jaca. My manager got an irate call from an executive huffing and puffing about a comment made on the show and why he had not been informed that I would be on Anele's show and …

At this point, Tumi switched off. This is why I was not made for being caged in an office or in a corporate environment: there are just too many people who play games that people like me, whose time is focused on personal hustle, have no interest in. I was mad as hell. As my mom would say, I saw red. You tell me what to say on air, I say it. You tell me what to say in the press, I say it. Now, in a space that is about me and my brand, which I have poured my soul into building, you want to dictate where, when and how I engage? No.

I lost it. I got so mad, I wrote a poem. Yeah, I know, that's gangsta, right? Got so mad, I wrote a poem. That only happens when I am so mad that I can't speak, so mad that, in that moment, I can't articulate what it is that's driving me mad. I climbed into bed, whipped out my phone and started typing. I wrote from the heart and with such clarity of thought that my heart and my head were in sync:

> *I can't breathe…*
> *I can't breathe with you hovering over my every word and measuring the spaces in which it echoes.*
> *I can't breathe when your need to watch your back makes you choke me and decide where the air goes.*
> *I can't breathe under the weight of patriarchy treating me like my resilience threatens you with anarchy.*
> *I can't breathe …*
> *stifled by the stench of your attitude towards me as an intellectual, three-dimensional being.*
> *I can't breathe …*
> *smothered by your smokescreen assurance whose tricks I'm already seeing.*

I can't breathe, you see, because you hold in your powerful white
hands the history dictated by a present that's hurting my future.

I can't breathe with this sharp pain squeezing my lungs, bleeding
from a divided land's infected sutures.

I can't breathe …

breathless from screaming and begging you to see me, not past me,
not a scorecard, not my kind, but me, Tumi.

I can't breathe with snipers fighting for a clear shot of my character to
assassinate me.

I can't breathe, sir, for swallowing my thoughts and washing them
down with yours. My brain lacks oxygen, numb from being dumbed
down.

I can't breathe from explaining why it is not OK to answer to you for
every single thing like a girl of three.

I can't breathe with the majesty of your institution towering over me;
I hold my breath and pray it doesn't swallow me.

I can't breathe because you inject a chill in me, a crippling loss of an
identity you won't allow me.

I can't breathe in this self-inflicted claustrophobia, reaching out to a
community that threw me in a box that just doesn't fit.

I can't breathe because all these words won't even matter a tiny bit, I
can't breathe but I can run and find my grit.

I can't breathe but I want to breathe, I need to breathe, I need to
catch my breath; you've exhausted me.

I am going to breathe because air is free and you cannot dictate when
I get to fill my lungs and feel the breeze.

I stole a breath, today, for my children, my country and mainly my
sanity. I reclaimed my breath and my spirit came to and I spoke my
truth with ease …

I can't breathe so I am breaking free from your chilly clutches and
your icy looks because I am tired of the brain freeze.

When I read this poem back to myself, I felt lighter. I felt as if I had
finally found the words to describe what I was going through at that time.
I also knew that I would be okay. I was not losing my mind, but I had
been playing *Minesweeper* at Jacaranda, and if I stayed it would only be a

matter of time before I hit another mine. There was no guarantee that I would survive the next one. I am at peace with not being a 'safe' black. When it is time to dial-a-darkie, I'm afraid I am permanently unavailable.

The only time I regretted leaving Jacaranda when I did was when Winnie Mandela died. Her passing was shattering, firstly because she was on my bucket list of people to meet. Secondly, because it felt like the death of the strongest female identity I knew in this country. She is such an important part of our history that her story should resonate in every corner of our land. Women who have to take on roles that challenge men. Women who debunk the idea that we are the weaker sex.

When I tweeted that I wished I was still working at Jacaranda when she passed, it was because I felt like I had given up on a fight before it had really begun. As if I had abandoned a cause. I had relinquished my right to speak up and to be in that space. The message that I don't belong and had allowed the system to win was driven home. I wished that, like her, I had stood strong and soldiered on.

11

I am not the dying type

When I moved to Johannesburg after being accepted at Wits, I felt like I was ready for the big city. I did not share the same fears as other small-towners; I had experienced violence, but it did not scare me. I figured I could handle petty crime. I just never imagined I would experience a hijacking.

A few months into my relationship with Mpho, we were hijacked. He was taking me back to res in his dad's Camry, when we stopped at a park just outside his friend's place in Edenvale. We had barely switched off the engine when the doors were flung open and two armed guys pulled us out of the car. In no time, there were four of them. They were clearly tripping on something, but the way they spoke threw me off.

On TV and in the movies, the hijackers usually speak broken English or some kind of township slang. These guys spoke the Queen's English and, I daresay, even had Model C accents. It was so ridiculous that I had to figure out if Mpho's friends were having a laugh or whether we were really being hijacked. Mpho tried to reason with them. I was just giggling.

The first thing they demanded was a gun; we told them we didn't have one. Then they wanted our cellphones and Mpho's shoes. I know, I don't get it either. One of the guys then took me away, pushing the gun against my neck. I wondered if this was take two of the rape scene, and whether someone would have to die this time. I started praying. Then the hijacker pushed me and I slid for a while before landing in water. I stayed there. I did not know what was happening with Mpho, and I didn't know what to do. I started giggling uncontrollably. *This was not happening.*

What felt like ages later, Mpho was also thrown into the water, all the while shouting for me. When he found me, we made our way out together. The giggles subsided and I broke down, fear eventually deciding to show up for the party. We made it to Sven's house and called Mpho's parents. When we got home, his mom ran me a bath with bath salts. I had no idea, until I sat in the bath, that the skin along my thigh had been scraped off as I was sliding down the ditch.

I jumped up, screaming, and cried like a baby. This experience would give me my first taste of insomnia. I kept seeing that man's eyes every time I tried to sleep; I heard their demands and their shouting. I felt for Mpho, who could not protect me and kept apologising for it.

The police, in all their professional glory, interrogated me on my own and implied that I was involved in the hijacking and had set Mpho up. I figured they either had a sick sense of humour or really wanted to see my ugly side. The car was found a month or so later, stripped, on the Mozambican border. A week after our hijacking, someone else was hijacked in the same area and killed. I prayed to God and thanked Him for sparing us. And I began to wonder what it was that was protecting me through all these trials.

I feel I have survived so much hectic stuff that whatever eventually kills me will probably be an anticlimax. Or, perhaps, to borrow Mama's words, I am 'not the dying type'.

In 2016 I received an email from Jaguar Land Rover in Menlyn. They were opening their newly refurbished dealership and wanted me to MC their event. While hobnobbing at the event, I met the dealer principal and a couple of the company's brand ambassadors. I joked about how cool it would be if they hooked me up with a Land Rover sponsorship. A couple of weeks later I received an email asking if I would be interested in driving one of Jaguar Menlyn's cars for the next couple of years, with reviews every six months.

I was not entirely comfortable with the idea, as I had read about celebrities whose sponsors would sever ties with them because they disagreed with their views or actions. I did not want to be kept in line, so I gave the offer careful consideration before I accepted. The status and style that the brand represented won me over.

Jaguar also seemed to like my public persona and what I represented in my comedy as a free-thinking South African. Their sponsorship would surely do wonders for my personal brand. About eight months into our relationship, the blowout happened at Jacaranda, and I was sure Jaguar would pull out. My critics were comparing me to Steve Hofmeyr, and I figured that if Jaguar bought that story, then they would not want to be associated with me – nobody wants to be linked to bigots or extremists. But Jaguar stood by me, and I reckoned if they could stand so strong amid all that condemnation, they would be with me for the long haul.

On 29 December 2017, Mpho and I were road-tripping with the kids between Gauteng and the Free State as part of an influencer campaign with South African National Parks (SANParks). It was a fantastic way to sell the experience of the national parks in the country, and the road trip was even sweeter in my sponsored Jaguar.

I must admit, though, I was still a bit uncomfortable travelling in a car that had my name on it, especially considering the social-media attacks after the Jacaranda blowout. It really is tragic how much idle time and disposable data people have on their hands.

We were to end our holiday in Sun City, which the kids had been promised as a reward for grinning and bearing nature and the wild with us. All they wanted was man-made madness and technology. Mpho and I swapped driving duties when we reached Johannesburg, and he took the wheel. On the R556 stretch about fifteen minutes outside Sun City, the kids were being rowdy and I scolded them for taking off their seat-belts. As they began to settle down, I went on my phone. Mpho was enjoying the drive and the music.

Just before the accident happened, I turned to Mpho and said I needed to go home to visit my mother's grave. Then I had my head down, focused on social media, when the car started bumping around. Mpho fought desperately to control the car, his hands firmly on the steering wheel. The children were scared, I was scared. I didn't know what was happening, but could only brace myself. I didn't have it in me to tell the kids to stop screaming. All I heard after that was screeching and a big bang.

I felt an impact, and then I was choking on smoke. I shut my eyes and braced myself for the next thing.

When I opened my eyes again, the worst was over. The car had stopped. The entire interior was covered in airbags – it looked like a smoke-filled marshmallow. I was trapped and screaming to be let out. I thought the car was on fire, and that I was burning too. As the dust cleared, I could see that Mpho and the kids were out of the car, but they were hardly audible. When the situation became clearer to me, I realised I could jump over and get out.

By then I heard a voice trying to get my attention via the speakers in the car. In the confusion, it took me a moment to understand what was going on – where the voice was coming from. A person from the call centre had picked up on the accident and was sending assistance. (I am still gobsmacked by the technology – a car that knows to call for help in an emergency!) I went on autopilot. It was not until I was out of the car that I saw another car was involved, and it looked pretty bad.

There had been a lot of holiday traffic on the road and people were flocking to the scene. My priority was my children. Mpho was in shock and not breathing properly. I scrambled for his asthma pump. Afia was crying. Someone was holding her – a stranger. Lesedi was staring quietly around him and Bonsu was rambling. I searched for juice to give them something sweet for the shock. A little later, Afia cried in Mpho's arms and then passed out. She stayed like that for so long, it scared me.

I called Osman and told him what had happened. He and his wife Shaaista arrived at the same time as the ambulance. I wanted to make my way to the other vehicle, but as Lesedi and Bonsu wanted to follow me, I held back.

The heat of the slowly setting sun beat down on us. I took a picture of the car. The looks on the faces of the bystanders made it obvious that they'd expected to see us much worse for wear. When a doctor came running to help us, I directed him to the other car. I did not know the extent of the injuries there, but I knew we did not need help as badly. By the time the ambulance arrived, I had been told things were really bad at the other car, and I knew the other car's passengers had to be prioritised. Our concerns were relatively minor: Lesedi's head was clearly hurt, Afia was out cold and Bonsu was limping.

I began to feel faint, but I refused to give in to the feeling, as it would freak my children out. I sat down and held them until Osman led us to the ambulance and began taking our belongings out of the car. I was trembling but relieved to be alive.

We all got into the ambulance along with a very badly injured woman, who was writhing and crying out in pain. Afia was asleep in Mpho's arms again and Bonsu sat in the front with the driver. Lesedi was in the back, watching the injured woman. He looked scared. I took him and placed his head on my chest so he wouldn't have to see that.

I did not know how many people had been in the other car, and if they were conscious. I was scared and prayed harder than I had ever prayed in my life. The paramedic was chatty, which helped take my mind off things. I encouraged his chatter, hoping it would also let the kids think things weren't that bad. Plus, it helpted to keep me conscious.

I don't know at which point I called my father-in-law, but Osman warned me that the news had broken on social media, so we would need to notify our families before it got to them the wrong way. Again, I found myself fading. I prayed for the injured woman and I held tightly onto my son. As I got out of the ambulance on reaching the hospital, I felt a sharp pain shoot up my back, but I was holding my kid so I sucked it up. I needed to make it to the casualty ward. By the time we got there, I had found my strength again.

I remember being asked to fill in some forms. Next thing, I was in a bed and on a drip. I asked for my children and wanted to know where my husband was. Eventually, the five of us were reunited on my bed. I remember feeling high, uncomfortable and extremely thirsty. I know I giggled with the staff – they were cracking jokes and asking for clues to the Secret Sound competition we were running on Jacaranda. On the other side of the curtain I could hear the driver of the other car ranting. I figured she was well within her rights to be angry.

Osman and Shaaista arrived to take us home. They had brought food for the children, cash and moral support. Both of them were extremely protective, as they had warned me that there was some animosity from the people in the other car. I had asked after them and had been advised to back off until they had calmed down; my concern would not have gone down well. I heeded this advice, and with all the stories these people later told the press, I don't regret doing so.

As the adrenalin wore off, pain started taking over. Even so, I refused to be admitted overnight, despite the doctor's recommendations. We discussed fitting a neck brace and undergoing a CT scan. I told the doctor that I would come back the next day for X-rays and that the medication was sufficient for now. I would get the brace outside the hospital and I would return for the scans. I could not bear the idea of my babies leaving the hospital without me.

The first week after the accident was torturous, but I had my family with me and my children could see me anytime they wanted. The rest I left to God. It turned out that I had absorbed most of the impact; it was my side of the car that had connected with the other car. The entire left side of my body was hit hard, as was Afia's. She walked with a limp for a few days after the accident. Lesedi could not sleep and, when he did, he had nightmares. In his five years of life I had never known him to suffer night terrors.

Bonsu was doing well, though. He had been hurt, but had processed everything in a logical way and was talking about it. The person I felt the most for was Mpho. He was on the phone every day with the husband of the badly injured woman in the other car. As we had been in the ambulance with her, we could not help but be concerned about her condition. Mpho was also trying to get access to the other people who had been involved in the accident, as we did not have any clear information about everyone else's injuries. We thought the compassionate thing to do after an accident would be to show concern for everyone involved.

It soon became apparent that the right wing was baying for blood. There were also people of colour who jumped on the bandwagon, in support of the people from the other car. And they, in turn, were spinning their own take on me and my part in the accident. You would think people wake up and plan accidents just so that they can screw up others' lives for fun. The playing ground was now a mess of casualties.

At the time of writing this book, the case was ongoing, so I cannot discuss what happened in that accident. All I can say is that I was not driving.

We went to see the badly injured woman after New Year's Eve. Her husband had discouraged us from visiting before then, saying the roads weren't safe with all the festivities going on. We took his advice. When we eventually went, we received a cold reception at first. As we started talking, the woman told me that she'd thought I did not care and she was not impressed. I explained my situation as best I could and I thought we had an honest conversation. After all, we were all still recovering and we had come to show our concern.

As with incidents in which high-profile people are involved, the accident became a juicy story for some journalists. One of them, Batlile Phaladi, wrote to Jaguar and claimed that I had been driving the car. She said that I was reckless and had been uncaring towards the victims of the accident. I mean, this was in her email:

- During the accident where Morake was driving a sponsored car, she was allegedly found at fault due to driving recklessly, is Jaguar aware of this?
- Victims have also contacted the paper saying that Morake did not show remorse after the accident, have Jaguar gotten in touch with victims?
- Due to the worrying numbers of fatalities on the road due to reckless driving, will Jaguar continue partnership with Morake?
- Is Jaguar still Morake's vehicle sponsor? If yes, why do you continue? If no, why did you decide to pull out?

'Due to the worrying numbers of fatalities' – I found it hard to believe this person really cared, but let's give her the benefit of the doubt. My nerves were already stretched to breaking point by the time this email was forwarded to me, and this was threatening to be the proverbial straw that would break my back. I loved the subtext of the email: 'Your brand is going to look like shit for continuing to sponsor this artist, so please let me be the first to know when you drop her so that I can feed the news to the tabloids.' (Oh no, I wasn't angry, not at all, hahaha.)

I felt as if I were under attack, so I googled her name to see if she was perhaps orchestrating a personal vendetta against me, or if I had become tabloid fodder. Based on the articles I found online, it seemed that Batlile Phaladi was a vulture who wrote bile about well-known people. I guess we all do what we must. In my most bitter moments, I comforted myself with the thought that Ms Phaladi would be stuck chasing deadlines and a per-word salary for the rest of her life, and I needed to stop taking this matter so personally.

However, I can't help but wonder if that email influenced Jaguar's decision not to renew my contract. The conversation changed from 'we are finalising insurance issues' to 'the renewal is under review'. I guess we'll never know. You win some, you lose some. My cousin reminded me that I had been wary of entering that relationship, as if I had known that this would happen, so my instincts were proven right and I should move on.

Move on I did. Regaining my anonymity was probably the biggest win; it had become a nuisance having the car announce my arrival wherever I went. Unlike with an ordinary car accident, where victims *only* need to deal with the law, their physical injuries and mental scars, I had to deal with more than I could cope with emotionally. I was overwhelmed, exhausted and at the end of all the fake bravado I could muster.

I asked my family to no longer call me about what they were reading in the papers. I had given them our version of events, and hearing what was being said elsewhere did not aid my recovery. On top of this, the idea of going back to Jacaranda had become even more challenging.

The people from Jaguar Menlyn, who had sponsored the car for the year, however, were supportive throughout. They offered me a car as soon as they found out we were okay and without transport hours away from home, and checked up on our progress. Their concern mattered to me, as I could feel a fire raging everywhere else.

So when Jaguar eventually decided to withdraw their sponsorship, I was okay with it. The car was never mine to begin with, and Jaguar had stood by me when the Tumigate shit hit the fan, so I could not take it personally.

My husband chose to leave me out of the ongoing legalities that were continuing as a result of the accident because, although the car was mine, I was not driving at the time of the accident. The fallout from the accident was only frustrating me and getting me into a froth. I had no control over what was happening, so I walked away.

12

I know I can go because you are okay

The first time I realised I could lose my mother was when she had an accident in which her car was written off. She was badly shaken but, like me when I had my accident, refused to be admitted to hospital. In her case, she came to regret it, as the whiplash caught up with her and she had to take time off work to recover. Two nights before her accident, I prayed for Mama with tears in my eyes. I'd woken up from a terrible nightmare, in which I'd dreamt that someone wanted her dead. When I told Mama this, she told me not to worry, but for the longest time she would remind me of how I had prayed for her and she had survived the accident, and to hold on to the power of prayer.

Mama did not have insurance, so her white Nissan Sentra ended up with backyard panelbeaters who said they could fix it, but never did. She never replaced the car, as she couldn't afford to. I was actually glad that she didn't. It forced her to begin using public transport, and because she was a people's person, this was a win for her in many ways. Now she could socialise from dusk till dawn; she made a new friend every week. I joked that I would make me a killing in donations at her funeral because of the number of people who would attend it. Years later, when I began working in entertainment, she said if I died, she looked forward to the large donations the celebrities would make at my funeral. We never talked about death seriously.

During the last month of Mama's life, I got to see her as she had been before. She was more lucid, had a wicked sense of humour and was absolutely smitten with my son. Mama refused to be a victim. At no point in her life did I hear her say, 'woe is me', or see her hang her head. She faced her adversities as challenges, things she needed to get past, rather than as hindrances.

When she died, her only regret, as far as I know, was not having opened the old-age home of which she had dreamt. Mama loved old people. She found value in them; she loved their gentleness, their vulnerability and their stubbornness. She had dreamt of establishing a facility that would take care of their medical needs and afford them a semi-luxurious lifestyle with good food, good company and lots of love. She wanted to invest her retirement package into this idea and partner with some people, but her mental health derailed her.

That nursing was Mama's vocation was clear. She was committed to all things healing and life-giving. In much the same way, I find that performing, especially live, is my vocation. I love connecting with people, and performing offers me a space where I can touch other people's lives, even if only briefly. Despite my love of performing, I am incredibly shy. I have to make a conscious effort to engage with people outside of my work environment. I always feel like I need an invitation to talk to strangers.

I enjoy pouring the best of me into my interaction with people, the downside being that there is a shamanic element to making people feel good, which can be exhausting. We absorb all those feelings from the audience, and they can literally weigh you down. So you need to purge them, to burp them out like Mama used to do when I massaged her. Much like those daily after-work massages I did for Mama, I, too, need relief sometimes from the energies that have sapped mine while I have been out doing what I am meant to do.

While Mama was alive but drifting further and further away from the woman I had known, I mourned her. She had been the centre of my life for so long. Of my sister and me, I think I had been the needier one. I was incredibly attached to Mama. When her mental breakdown happened, she and I had to switch roles. Even though I was still in high school, I had to become more responsible, not only for myself, but also for my mother. I had to take care of her, even if I was so ill-equipped.

I did not know what to do with this woman who was being defeated by the chemistry in her brain. I kept expecting her to pull herself together – to sort out her medication and nutrition. The woman I knew was supposed to beat this condition. She was a fighter, not someone who would succumb to a manageable illness. But she struggled, and I often felt like a powerless spectator. Mama had been there for me at every turn, yet here I was, useless at being there for her.

When I became financially stable, I threw money at the problem. I found her a psychiatrist in Johannesburg. Mama wanted to get back into nursing, but in the private sector. I began the process of re-registering her with the Nurses Council. I wanted my mother back, not this woman withering away before my eyes. I got frustrated with her and with myself.

My frustration with her stemmed from when she had worked as a psychiatric nurse and shared stories of people functioning despite their mental illnesses, and how educated people often got so much further because they took the time to understand their illnesses. She was intelligent. She was educated. What the heck was her problem? I felt as if she had decided that someone had done this to her, and whoever that person was had won. I was reminded of the nightmare I'd had in which someone was trying to kill her; it had turned into a sinister reality.

And I was frustrated with myself, because I did not know *how* to help her. Half the time I pretended she wasn't ill, as if by refusing to acknowledge her illness I would somehow make it disappear. I watched this woman, who always took so much pride in her appearance, care less and less about it. I could always tell when it was about to happen, when she'd decide that taking care of herself was too much effort and she wasn't even going to try. I would force her to go out with me, knowing that she would have to bathe and put herself together. When I left to go to university in Johannesburg, it meant I wouldn't be there to do that. So she deteriorated quietly, until eventually my uncle decided she would be better off surrounded by family. From then on, they took care of her.

Mama used to disappear for days on end, and I would not be able to sleep. I had my first anxiety attack in the early 2000s, when she had been missing for a week during a manic episode and nobody had any idea where she was. I feared the worst. She was living in the Free State while I was chasing a degree in Joburg.

Luckily, I have always dated older or mature men, so my boyfriend at that time was a senior who did not hesitate to call me out if I was losing focus. He was a good shoulder to cry on when my mother was on one of her bipolar highs and I was worried sick. During first and second year, I partied only when my boyfriend was present and I delivered good academic results. He and I had a good relationship to start with, but it ended badly and Mama held me every night when I cried after the break-up.

She would comfort me by assuring me that there was a whole queue of men who would love to love and value me. She was mad as hell that this guy had broken my heart. And I loved her for it. My ex recently sent me a message on the anniversary of Mama's passing, and he asked me if I wanted to know what Mama had said to him after we broke up. He started off by saying, 'Your mom spoke her mind. She was a good woman.'

I told him not to tell me what she'd said, because I have a good idea what it was. I am sure that she had made it very clear how badly he had hurt me, and how she had a good mind to kick his ass. Besides, I didn't want to die of embarrassment if she'd said anything worse.

After the break-up, Mama gave me money and sent me away to my aunt's place for the rest of the holidays so I wouldn't have to see my ex. I drank up that money with my cousins and had a fantastic end to the December break. My mother understood me in a way nobody else does. She knew when to be there for me and when to leave me alone.

In 2011 she was admitted to hospital after medication she was taking conflicted with the lithium for her bipolar disorder. I pulled out of a gig and drove to Thaba Nchu as soon as I got the call. Mama wasn't speaking, but she was conscious. But she couldn't eat or move – she just lay there.

I was afraid of Mama when I saw her – I did not recognise her. She had lost weight and looked ten years older, but still had the same braids in her hair that she'd got the last time she visited me some months before. A distant cousin, now also deceased, helped me undo her braids. According to our culture, when someone is sick, we aren't allowed to cut their hair. I reasoned that as these were braids, technically it wasn't her hair. I got an earful from my uncle when he arrived and discovered the braids in a bin – was I trying to kill his sister? He was overwrought and scared. I understood why. He had watched his wife pass away years ago, and now my mother was in a similar situation. I let him vent, but I finished the job.

When I got to my Aunty Benny's house, where I was staying during my visit, I sat in the car and prayed. I begged God to spare my mother's life. I did not know what His plans were, but I was not ready for her to go. Mama was moved to a semi-private hospital in Bloemfontein, and I became more hopeful. We made the drive there every day. She was making unintelligible sounds when she wanted to speak, but she seemed quite determined to say something. I could not bear to see her like that.

When I left her ward to get something from the car, I found the nurses at the nurses' station discussing me. They stopped me and asked me for a photograph. My heart lined up a row of expletives, but my head called off the dogs and I politely asked them to give me a moment to collect myself. They asked if that was my mother in there, and I told them that it was. They realised that they'd made a faux pas and backed off.

My mother was on dialysis as her kidneys had shut down; her body was a toxic wasteland. The doctor treating her said that they were cleaning her blood to clear it of the poison that had been created by the combination of medications in her system. Whoever had prescribed the medication she was on had either not known she was on lithium or had made a terrible mistake.

After the dialysis, my mother began to make a slow recovery. Only then did I return to my home in Johannesburg, with the intention of visiting her again the following weekend. At least she was talking and eating, albeit puréed food, but eating nonetheless.

I regularly returned to Thaba Nchu to see my mother and she looked better each time; she was even refusing to stay in bed. After a corporate gig in Bloemfontein, I took my hired car and visited her at home. She was lucid and jonesing for fish and chips, so I thought her life was about to take a major turn for the better.

We bought takeaway at Captain DoRegos. Listen, when you are in a small town, your options are limited, okay, and this was her favourite joint for such delicacies. We then drove to Aunty Benny's house, where Mama shared her fish and chips before I rushed her back home so I could make my flight back to Johannesburg. That was in May.

In June, I saw her alive for the last time. I found her bedridden once again, but her face was fuller and she spoke like the woman who had raised me. After thirteen years of seeing Mama at the polar opposites of her bipolar disorder, she was now a sober-minded, cheeky Tebza. I even asked her if her mind was compensating for the knock her body had taken. Yes, we were still that candid in our conversations.

Mama was weak, though, and had to be physically turned, was in adult nappies and struggling to eat. She sent me out for her favourite juice – apricot Liqui-Fruit – but could barely drink it, finding it too sweet. My Aunt Mamogolo said she had complained that food was too salty as well, even when they gave her something bland.

I had brought Bonsu with me, and Mama's face lit up when she saw him. He sat on the bed and they had their gibberish conversation and sang their Rihanna song. I wanted to stay longer, but Mpho had been calling to ask when I'd be home, and I had promised to be back by Sunday afternoon. We had planned family time with his folks and his sister. I told him I would miss it. He got annoyed. I got annoyed. Which part of 'my mother is not well' had he missed?

Perhaps he assumed she was recovering and did not understand why I wanted to stay on. I decided to linger for a few hours longer, but Mama told me to go home to my husband. She said that she knew I was fine, that I was in good hands, with people who loved me. She kept asking after my sister, who was in town but could not be reached. I told her that Vonani was fine, she was back in school and working part-time. 'As long as she finishes school,' my mother said. Even on what turned out to be her deathbed, she was concerned about her daughter's education.

Three days later, I was told that she had taken a turn for the worse and I should come home as soon as possible. I made plans to go that weekend, but from Wednesday evening into early Thursday morning on 23 June, I struggled to sleep and I had an unfamiliar feeling in the pit of my stomach. I woke up with a start in the wee hours of the morning, as if someone had shaken me awake.

Mpho found me sitting up and asked what was wrong. I told him I needed to go home to Mama. Later that morning, as I got ready to drop my son off at crèche, my cousin called, and before she could tell me what had happened, I asked her if Mama had died. She sighed and said yes. My world slipped off its axis. It was an 'everything stopped' experience.

Vonani was in the other room, playing with Bonsu. Adele's 'Someone Like You' was playing loudly in the background; it was still an anthem at the time. I asked my sister to sit down, and delivered the news. She immediately broke down, holding onto my son, who became scared. I rushed to get some water for Vonani, at no point stopping to feel sorry for myself. I called Mama-in-law and she promised to come over with my father-in-law.

Every time I told someone of Mama's passing, the reality sank in, and the tears came. I called Arepp to cancel a read-through and rehearsal for a show I was directing for them. I called the comedy club; I could no longer take my spot that weekend. Then I called my management – they would have to contact anyone I had missed. I could feel the strength leave me, the panic rising in my chest and a headache starting, as if someone was squeezing my head at the temples. I could not reach my husband, I realised, my heart sinking, because he had forgotten his phone at home. Today of all days. I began to unravel.

I called my father, who told me to be strong. I found him so cold. Prison must have done that to him. His daughter was telling him her mother, his ex-wife, was dead, and all he could tell her was to be strong. Yeah, man, fuck apartheid and all its architects; it cost me a father. I hung up. I knew Mpho's parents would give me the warmth I needed in that moment. Vonani was a mess, and someone had to hold her up. That some-one was me. For the life of me, I don't know what happened to Bonsu through all of this, but I think his nanny took him to school. I was in no state to take him anywhere.

As soon as Mama-in-law held me, grief overtook me and I wailed in a way I had never done before. I did not recognise my own voice. I suddenly felt scared, like a child lost in a shopping mall with no sign of her mother. I would never find her, hear her, see her again.

Mama had been ill for some time, and the time she spent on her back in hospital and at home had led to her contracting pneumonia. It was this fight that she lost, in the end. Mama was intelligent and a nurse; she knew the signs were there, and she went out of her way to hide them from us. She hid food under the mattress cover to hide the fact that she couldn't eat, and had been manipulating her medical file throughout her bipolar treatment.

Mama was too smart for her own good. She had refused all efforts to take her to hospital, so no one realised she had pneumonia; they just knew something was horribly wrong. The day before she finally left for the hospital, the last thing she said to my grandmother was, 'I am going away to die.' Thank goodness my grandmother, ninety-two at the time, was hard of hearing.

My deepest regret is never asking Mama about her time in prison. She wasn't there for long, but some kind of trauma could explain her chemical imbalance. We spoke about deep things, my mom and I. I asked her about the time she lost my baby brother, how it had felt, what she must have gone through. She had felt the baby die in her womb, she said, even though the scan showed a heartbeat. A week later, she delivered a still-born baby. She buried him, cried at his grave and moved on.

I asked her whether she had ever considered seeing a therapist after everything she had experienced – losing her baby, the time in prison, the divorce, Papa Henry's passing. Her response was that she was just a simple Motswana woman who got on with her life. I began to wonder if Mama would have unravelled if she'd sought help. I wish I could say that I was as stoic as Mama when I had to let her go.

On the drive to Thaba Nchu, I did not see the road, I just saw myself arrive at the gate. I looked at Mama's bedroom window, waiting for her to pull the curtain back and look straight at me before emerging at the door. I walked in to find the house dimly lit with candles. I did not dare enter her bedroom. My grandmother, very old, beautiful, eyes almost closed from the wrinkles on her face, sat in her usual spot on her bed. She was staring out of the window, as though in quiet dialogue with God.

I greeted her, fighting back the tears. She told me that this was my time to show that I was a woman. I nodded. She reassured me that my mother was finally at peace; she had suffered enough. My uncle was there, mask-ing his pain with his loud voice and inappropriate jokes. I tell you, I was genetically gifted with badly timed humour. Only when we gathered in the lounge to pray did I give in to the pain.

Bonsu was two at the time. He kept going to my mother's room, look-ing for his grandma and singing their song, 'Oh nana, what's my name'. This child was breaking me.

I barely slept that night. The following day we went coffin shopping. It was so bizarre, looking at coffins and wondering which one Mama would like. I tried to conjure up an image of all the coffins she had been impressed with at other funerals and picked something along those lines. The guy assisting me was going on and on about the soft lining and material, and I was like, 'Dude, I'm sure she won't mind.'

We looked at tombstones. I picked one in the shape of a Bible, because it symbolised more than that: my mother loved books and raised us to love books, so she would have a book as her tombstone. It also had to have space for my uncle's details, as she would be buried on top of his grave. He had been buried long ago, in the early 1990s.

Part of the funeral arrangements was the washing of the body. My aunts did this; I could not bear it. However, I had some embalming oil from a trip to Egypt, and I wanted to use it all on her. I had picked out the dress she wore at my wedding for her to be buried in. The cream colour would be appropriate, I reckoned. Then I kissed her goodbye. She looked as if she might say something; perhaps her spirit had not quite left her body yet.

The next time I saw my mother was in my grandmother's bedroom. This time all I saw was a husk. Not my mother, just her body. I have no memory of that body. I may have shut it out or my heart chose to remember a living person.

I coped well enough at the funeral, until the moment they began lowering the coffin into the ground. My belly button ached, and I begged them to stop. I was not ready to let her go, but they did not listen. Her favourite hymn, 'Sedi la ka', was sung. I began gasping, choking on air. A part of me went down with her; the rest is a haze. I did not know real pain until I lost my mother. When I think back to my aching belly button, I recall a conversation we'd had when I wanted a belly ring in high school. Mama asked me not to pierce my belly button, because that was where I had been connected to her when I was in her womb, and it was really special to her. So I never messed with my belly button.

A year after my mother's passing, I hosted a special lunch at my grandmother's place. I invited her siblings and asked one of them to prepare my mother's favourite food. We reminisced about the good times with Mama. My grandmother told me that I would have to bury *her* – her children all seemed to be leaving before her. Of the nine, only three remained. I told her she was not going anywhere. She said, '*Nee man, ek is moeg, ek wil ook gaan. Ke emetse hela gore Modimo a ntseye.'* (No man, I am tired, I also want to go. I am just waiting for the Lord to take me.)

A month later, my grandmother passed away peacefully in her sleep. I felt my mother sitting next to me at her funeral service. I haven't felt such a definite presence of my mother since, and it made me feel at peace. I took my grandmother's passing better. She had lived a full life, for nearly a century. This time, death's timing made sense. When I go home to my grandmother's house nowadays, it is to reconnect. It is to rejuvenate my soul and remember.

'I know I can go because you are okay.'

Those were the last words Mama said to me. I disagreed with her; I was never ready to let her go. But *she* was ready to go. I have always used her faith in me as fuel when my own faith is waning. Mama always remarked on my ability to pray and the power of my prayers. She knew this skill had been passed onto me by my grandmother.

When I see myself wanting to repeat Mama's mistakes, I catch myself as if she were there in that moment, chastising me. I may not be getting everything right, but when my spirit is compromised, I will fight to protect it. It is all I have – my soul. I do not have Bonang Matheba's looks or Oprah Winfrey's money. I only have me, my intelligence and my love for what I do. If I lose my spirit, I lose my ability to continue serving the best way I know how.

I still refuse to grow up, I refuse to give in, and half the time I forget how old I am. Bonsu got me into Dr. Seuss books, and there is a quote that has stuck with me from *Oh, The Places You'll Go!*: 'You have brains in your head, you have feet in your shoes. You can steer yourself any direction you choose.'

Oh boy, have I gone in interesting directions! And I do not regret a single one. My brain is still fairly intact and my feet are itching for adventure. I do not know when my time on this earth will be up, but I intend on using that time productively. I will no longer keep depositing the best of me into ventures that leave me at an intellectual and emotional deficit. I am worth so much more, and I need to stop being afraid of telling myself that. I have learnt over time that, yes, humility is important, but you have to value yourself so as not to end up at the bottom of the food chain.

I took a detour by stepping into radio, a space where I got to be a rookie again. I was in a position of learning and being led, as opposed to leading: from being my own boss to having people I had to answer to. Now, I am back on a journey of discovery and continuation – I am back to saying the unsaid in the comedy space, to creating film and to playing in that mesmerising-yet-far-from-lucrative space called television. (In South Africa, I find that the pay never matches the input. It is great for reaching the masses, though, and I love my masses.)

I still dream about my mother. Sometimes, the dreams are just brain activity; at other times, they speak to my situation and guide me. I speak to Mama whenever I feel her presence. As long as my belly button exists, that bond is still there. When I reach a milestone, I hear her saying with pride, 'My dear, you are a trier.'

The blind faith she had in me gave me momentum when I was a bright-eyed matriculant about to face Big Bad Johannesburg. It made me believe that there was no reason why I couldn't make it in the entertainment industry. I believe I still have so much going for me. I continue to fill my gratitude journal with both the massive and miniscule blessings I receive. It is my moment to keep up with God and with myself.

I have never been a Bible-bashing Christian, but I was raised by a God-loving grandmother who taught me one thing: you go down on your knees and you pray to God. She gave me the same advice whether I was going through tough times or announcing great news. You go down on your knees and you pray to God. That is the constant that has got me through the worst. I have never set out to hurt anyone, walk over people or impede someone from reaching their destiny.

When I have come under attack, I have taken full responsibility for my role, and have never assumed the position of victim. I can never do that. It would be an insult to the blood, sweat and tears of my mother and grandmother. They raised me to be steadfast in my faith and to always hold my head high. I cannot walk with my head down, otherwise my crown will slide off.

In my weakest moment, when everything had come to a head and I was speaking with the voice of a defeated black woman, Rethabile Ramaphakela scolded me. She is one of the smartest and hardest-working women I know. Her independence and relentless ambition remind me of

Mama Mpho, mom's bestie. Rethabile told me the story of her grand-mother, who said, 'Don't let them steal your crown.' They do not deserve what you have worked hard for, suffered for and have a right to. They cannot have your peace. It is not theirs to take.

I am learning to protect my peace better. To laugh as hard and as loud as I ever have, and to live in service to humanity, whatever that means to a simple Motswana girl like me.